D. MICHAEL QUINN

D. Michael Quinn

D. MICHAEL QUINN
MORMON HISTORIAN

GARY TOPPING

SIGNATURE BOOKS | 2022 | SALT LAKE CITY

The opinions expressed in this book are not necessarily those of the publisher.

Design by Jason Francis.

FIRST EDITION | 2022

LIBRARY OF CONGRESS CATALOGING-IN-PUBLICATION DATA

Names:	Topping, Gary, 1941– author.
Title:	D. Michael Quinn : Mormon historian / Gary Topping.
Description:	First edition.	Salt Lake City : Signature Books, 2022.	Summary: "D. Michael Quinn (1944–2021) was one of Mormonism's greatest historians, though his books have profound relevance to Utah and western history as well. After completing his doctorate in history at Yale University in an almost unprecedented three years, he taught at Brigham Young University from 1976 to 1988. His attraction to difficult themes in Mormon history drew controversy which led to resignation from his academic position and eventual excommunication from the Church of Jesus Christ of Latter-day Saints. His large, elaborately documented books, such as his three volumes on the Mormon hierarchy and his Early Mormonism and the Magic World View, set a new standard for Mormon historical scholarship"— Provided by publisher.
Identifiers:	LCCN 2021048013 (print)	LCCN 2021048014 (ebook)	ISBN 9781560854449 (paperback)	ISBN 9781560854159 (ebook)
Subjects:	LCSH: Quinn, D. Michael, 1944–2021.	Brigham Young University—Faculty—Biography.	Church of Jesus Christ of Latter-day Saints—Historiography.	Religion historians—United States—Biography.	Mormon gays—Biography.	Ex-church members—Church of Jesus Christ of Latter-day Saints— Biography.	Mormon Church—Historiography.	LCGFT: Biographies.
Classification:	LCC BX8695.Q46 T67 2022 (print)	LCC BX8695.Q46 (ebook)	DDC 289.3092 [B]—dc23/eng/20211013
	LC record available at https://lccn.loc.gov/2021048013 LC ebook record available at https://lccn.loc.gov/2021048014

For Marianna

CONTENTS

ACKNOWLEDGMENTS

This book would not have existed without Gary James Bergera, managing director of the Smith-Pettit Foundation. In fact, the idea was his; when he asked me to consider writing it, I protested that I thought myself unqualified. The reader will have to judge which of us was right. Gary even provided me with access to vast files of primary and secondary sources that he had been collecting over the years, and which are now housed at Signature Books Publishing. Gary could have written the book, but since he didn't and I did, I accept full responsibility for its contents.

Since I had never written a book about a living person, I was uncertain what level of involvement I should seek from Quinn. I knew of his impatience with criticism, though I saw later that most of the criticisms that aroused his ire would have vexed anyone. So I initially decided I would spare myself the pressure of having him looking over my shoulder, write the book as I wanted to write it, then seek his factual corrections only after I was finished. Once I began, though, I realized that I was going to need his help in untangling the family relations of his childhood, so I sought him out. I found him immensely helpful, and my early chapters are much improved as a result. I needed him less when I got to his mature years, for which relatively elaborate documentation exists. Sadly, Quinn passed away unexpectedly as this book was nearing completion.

I also drew upon reminiscences of a few of Quinn's friends. Although my conversations with Gary Bergera, Ron Priddis, Newell G. Bringhurst, and Brian Cannon do not appear in my footnotes, they underlie my observations throughout the later chapters. Melissa Coy generously provided access to her JSTOR account at Westminster College's Giovale Library where I could find book reviews. Quinn's children (Mary, Lisa, and Moshe) kindly allowed references and quotations from their father's unpublished autobiographical writings.

Finally, the wisdom, encouragement and editorial expertise of my wife, Marianna Hopkins, are in silent evidence here as in almost everything else I have written.

PROLOGUE

By the late 1980s, D. Michael Quinn's career as a rising star in the firmament of Mormon historical studies was still in ascent. For almost twenty years, the trajectory of that career had amazed virtually all who observed it. Already in adolescence he had begun reading the standard works of Mormon history, indexing and making notes on them. As an undergraduate at Mormon-owned Brigham Young University, he made a false start as a pre-med major, then graduated with honors in English and philosophy.

But history was always his true passion. When, in the late 1960s, the Church of Jesus Christ of Latter-day Saints, under the leadership of apostles and official Church Historians Joseph Fielding Smith and Howard W. Hunter, began to open its archives freely to all comers, Quinn was a constant visitor. With his rapid typing speed and long workdays, he compiled volumes of typed transcriptions and notes on the papers of Mormon leaders and organizations whose papers had never before seen the light of day.

In 1972, when Leonard J. Arrington took charge as the new Church Historian of the newly created History Division at the church headquarters and began assembling a staff mostly of young scholars, Quinn's monkish work ethic and almost preternaturally deep knowledge of Mormon history caught Arrington's attention. Later, working on a master's degree in the University of Utah history department, Quinn was employed as a research assistant to Davis Bitton, who was Assistant Church Historian to Arrington. Quinn's work excelled both in quality and quantity, and Arrington confided that he wanted to prepare Quinn as his possible successor, helping to engineer his acceptance to a PhD program at Yale University under the great western historian Howard R. Lamar.

Quinn completed his doctoral program in three years. His Yale University dissertation, like his master's thesis, focused on his life-long interest in the development of the ecclesiastical hierarchy of the Mormon Church, and won a best dissertation award.

Back in Utah, Quinn earned a position on the history faculty at Brigham Young University, rising, within a few years, to full professor and director of the graduate program. As successful in teaching as in research, he developed a cadre of devoted students who voted him a best teacher award. His personal life, too, was going well: a happy marriage had produced a family of two daughters and two sons. As for his church life, he had already successfully filled a two-year proselytizing mission in England and served in the bishopric while in graduate school, among other lay positions.

And yet, a historical meteorologist with a good weather eye might have seen thunder clouds on the horizon. Quinn's first book, a study of the ecclesiastical career of J. Reuben Clark, longtime member of the church's governing First Presidency, had been reviewed well enough, but it had been a church-sponsored project, and Quinn had felt compelled to temper some of his judgments of the controversial Clark's policies.

From there, things began to go downhill. While his next book, *Early Mormonism and the Magic World View*, sold well for a densely documented scholarly work, it drew thunderclaps of denunciation from conservative Mormons, in particular the Foundation for Ancient Research in Mormon Studies (FARMS), a non-profit foundation devoted to the conservative, literal interpretation of Mormon scriptures and to the church as divinely created and unsullied in its history by imperfect humans. Quinn's marriage succumbed to simmering tensions resulting, in part, from his homosexual orientation. BYU let him know that further support for his controversial research interests would not be forthcoming and his continuance on the faculty would require his confinement to "safe" topics. Rather than accommodate, he resigned from BYU and eventually left the state, but continued to do battle with conservative members of the hierarchy who attacked his scholarly integrity. On September 26, 1993,

Quinn received notice of his excommunication from the Mormon church, joining five others who had been cut off that same month.

How could such a stellar career have so quickly come to such an impasse? This brief biography attempts, in part, to answer that question.

CHAPTER ONE

AMBIGUOUS IDENTITIES

Childhood and adolescence, for most people, are difficult times at best, but Dennis Michael Quinn had to cope with challenges from which many are spared. A broken family, less than effective parenting, excruciating physical problems, ambiguous ethnic, social, and religious identities, and a developing same-sex attraction—all of these forced the boy to rely upon the proverbial resiliency of childhood, a resiliency that the cruelties of our adult world and the tribulations of Nature too often compel our children to exercise.

Some of the ambiguities of the world into which he was born on March 26, 1944, in Pasadena, California, were relatively easily resolved. Others were troubling and lingered into adulthood. One was his ethnic identity, for his father was Mexican-American and his mother was Anglo-Swiss.

A proverb of the civil rights movement of the 1960s held that one cannot be proud of whom one is, because no one can control that. The goal is not to be ashamed. Daniel Peña, Quinn's father, was ashamed of his Mexican identity and went to extraordinary pains to repudiate it. Though born in Arizona of Mexican immigrant parents, he grew up in the *barrio* of East Los Angeles, speaking, at first, only Spanish. One of his boyhood friends was Anthony Quinn, who later became the celebrated movie star. Quinn, too, was of mixed ethnic identity: his father, Franklin "Frank" Quinn, was an Irish immigrant to Mexico who married a Mexican woman.[1] Unlike Peña, though, Quinn's father's name allowed him to conceal his ethnicity when

---

1. See Anthony Quinn, *The Original Sin: A Self-portrait by Anthony Quinn* (Boston: Little Brown & Co., 1972), chap 2.

1

convenient (though his swarthy complexion allowed him famously to play characters of various ethnicities during his acting career). Seeking a similar shortcut to assimilation, Peña changed his name to Quinn and appropriated his friend's story of Irish ancestry as his own. Although the boyhood friendship soon dissolved, the name and the falsified identity endured.

For some reason, Peña thought that changing his name to Donald at the same time further facilitated the ethnic deception. To deepen the subterfuge, he married Joyce Workman, a blue-eyed redhead of Irish appearance, and told his wife that his fictional "Spanish" mother was dead. Shortly after the birth of their only son, Dennis Michael, Peña came clean about at least part of the tale: during a drive into what was for Joyce a totally unfamiliar part of the Los Angeles *barrio*, they stopped in front of a house she had never seen and he took her inside to introduce her to his actual Mexican mother. Topping off what must have been an unsettling experience for Joyce, the old woman whispered to her, while Donald had briefly left the room, "I feel so sorry for you."[2]

The deception, of which the boy Michael[3] became aware at an early age, became a factor in the distant nature of his relationship with his father, a distance which continued until being mitigated slightly just before the latter's death. In the introduction to his diary of a sojourn in Chiapas of several months in 1999, Quinn makes the nature of his relationship with his father clear:

> Although I began telling others of my Mexican ancestry as a teenager, I've never made any effort to recapture it. Aside from a couple of hours in Tijuana with my wife and children when I was nearly thirty, I've never been to Mexico until today. I wasn't interested in learning Spanish, but eagerly studied German. I've lived in both Germany and Austria, while maintaining a decades-long fantasy of seeking Swiss citizenship, because my mother's grandmother was a native of Bern. During four years of residence in Europe, I never went to Spain but fell

---

2. D. Michael Quinn, "Journal/Journey of a Gringo Chicano in Mexico," 1, unpublished manuscript in my possession; Quinn, telephone conversation with Gary Topping, Apr. 28, 2020.

3. Although Quinn continued to use the name Dennis throughout childhood, he was "D. Michael Quinn" during his maturity, and from this point I designate him either as "Michael" or "Quinn" to avoid confusion.

in love with Italy. I've often hoped to visit the pyramids of Egypt, but had far less interest in the pyramids of Mexico. During the past month, when friends expressed the assumption that I'm moving to Mexico to "get back to your roots," I told them I would prefer to live anywhere except Latin America. Despite being Chicano, I'm a Gringo in attitude and experience.[4]

That ambiguous identity even affected his professional life. In 1974, while a graduate student at Yale, Quinn's application for a Ford Foundation grant based on the applicant's Mexican-American status was turned down. His graduate advisor, Howard R. Lamar, learned that the rejection was justified, despite Quinn's Mexican heritage, by the facts that he did not have a Spanish surname and did not speak Spanish. "An ultimate compliment for my father's decision to become WASP," he noted, with evident bitterness. "Never told Dad about this consequence of his American success story."[5]

If Donald Quinn's mother had felt sorry for his wife's being married to such a master of deception, she might have felt even sorrier for her grandson when he arrived, for the little boy became a pawn in a religious tug of war between his Catholic father and his maternal grandmother, "Nana," a ferociously devout Mormon. That such a war should develop was a strange circumstance, for Donald Quinn was a classic case of a "nominal" Catholic. When he married Joyce Workman, a sixth generation Mormon, he attended Mormon services with her and consented to have their son raised in her church. Later, after their divorce, he married a Baptist and compliantly attended church with her, thus branding himself as about as nominal a Catholic as one would ever expect to find.

Nevertheless, D. Michael Quinn remembers existing in more of a Catholic environment than a Mormon one, for his father's relatives were more numerous than his Mormon ones, and whether or not their Catholicism was any more devout than his father Donald's, they were at least *there*. And Nana took exception to the

---

4. Quinn, "Journal/Journey," 1. This introduction to the journal is undated; subsequent citations to it will be given by date.

5. D. Michael Quinn, "Chosen Path: A Gay Chicano's Odyssey in Mormon History," entry for 1974, unpublished memoir in possession of Signature Books Publishing, Salt Lake City. My source is the version of Quinn's memoir dated June 1998. In the years since 1998, Quinn continued to revise and expand his autobiography.

Catholic influence, making strenuous efforts to see that the Mormonism dominated. Even something as seemingly innocent as a family dinner became a religious battleground. Rather than allow the Catholics to recite their simple prayer over the food—"Bless us, O Lord, and these thy gifts which we are about to receive through thy bounty"—Nana insisted that little Dennis give a long, elaborate, and improvised Mormon prayer. When he was finished, she would glare at Donald, as if to say, "See? That's what a proper prayer sounds like."[6] It was a situation calculated to turn the young boy against all religion. Amazingly, perhaps despite rather than because of his grandmother's heavy-handed ways, he developed a solid commitment to Mormonism that would sustain him through some of the roughest treatment his co-religionists could hand out.

Quinn's parents' divorce when he was about five years old gave rise to another ambiguity in his life: who were his real parents? Obviously he knew biologically who they were, but the more difficult question of who was going to assume the parenting role came increasingly to the fore. His father had visitation rights, but he exercised them only sporadically and ineffectually. He would suddenly show up for an afternoon approximately once a month and take the boy to a movie or a similar entertainment, brief encounters that hindered development of real father-son bonds, and Quinn remembered no actual heart-to-heart talks. Quinn and his mother lived with her parents, and his grandfather was similarly unreachable emotionally. Unquestionably the dominant figure in his rearing was Nana, his grandmother. An emotionally needy person herself, she made a strenuous effort to function, not as grandmother, but as mother. She tried to convince Quinn, that although biologically he was his mother's son, in a spiritual sense he belonged to Nana as a reincarnated spirit of a baby she had miscarried in her fifth pregnancy. Accordingly, the boy's relationship with his mother diminished in warmth—Nana taught him to regard her daughter as only "a sister or a friend"—while he wrote deeply affectionate letters to Nana on her birthday and other anniversaries.[7]

Further, Nana exhibited a general hatred of men. Her father had beaten her, and her grandfather had made sexual advances. Thus she

---

6. Quinn, telephone conversation with Topping.
7. Quinn, "Chosen Path," 11–12.

encouraged the boy to hate his own father and grandfather—for their maleness as well as their Catholicism. The not unexpected result of Nana's pressures was that the boy grew up with difficulties in developing intimacy: "Nana's hatred and fears stunted my ability to trust and believe in myself or be intimate with anyone."[8]

Nana did encourage his trust and reverence for Mormon Church leaders. "As I grew up, LDS church leaders were my only role model for assertive males and the only alternative I had against my grandmother's hatred of men."[9] It is an astonishing disclosure, given Quinn's battles with that very LDS hierarchy during his adult years and the exposure of their human failings in his immense trilogy that we will later examine in some detail. And it helps to indicate some of the disappointment and frustration his eventual excommunication at the hands of the men he once looked up to must have brought.

A third ambiguity was Quinn's social class. Although born in Pasadena, he grew up in a working-class neighborhood in Glendale. There was a trailer park nearby, and the railroad tracks were only a block away. The proximity of the railroad was an important symbol of the fact that he was very conscious of living on the proverbial "wrong side of the tracks." There was no Mormon ward (congregation) in his neighborhood, so he attended a ward some four miles away, which happened to be in an affluent neighborhood. As a consequence, he grew up with a feeling of trying to fit into a social class to which he did not actually belong. Further, the neighborhood school that he was supposed to attend was not very good, so the Quinns lied about their address in order to register at a school in the same affluent neighborhood as his ward. Eventually the family was able to relocate into that neighborhood, but the class ambiguity remained everpresent.[10]

The deepest ambiguity in his youth, however, was his struggle to understand and to accommodate his emerging sexual identity. His first awareness of that identity came at age eight in a Mormon baptismal font. It was arranged that his uncle would perform the baptism, and as the two undressed, Quinn experienced his first

---

8. Quinn, "Chosen Path," 12.
9. Quinn, "Chosen Path," 12.
10. Quinn, "Chosen Path," 16, 21.

closeness to another male body and felt a certain sexual stirring. The stirring intensified as the man took the boy into his arms and lowered him into the warm water in what he considered to be a same sex embrace. To heighten the ambiguity even further, at the very moment he was experiencing his first homosexual experience, he felt a deep spiritual experience as well: "In the embrace of a man for the first time I could remember, I felt a burning within me of what I knew was God's presence."[11]

At the same time, Quinn began having sexual opportunities among the teenage boys in the Aaronic Priesthood quorum in his Mormon ward. In fact, it is surprising to read in his memoir the number and frequency of such instances that he observed as well as participated in. In an attempt to comprehend what was going on, he went to the city library, where he looked up, first of all, "pervert," which led him to "abnormal psychology, homosexuality." And there it was: "I now knew the name for what was wrong with me." Knowledge did not bring relief, but rather despair: "Everything I read was negative," he recalled. "I wanted to die and sometimes thought of jumping in front of speeding cars as I walked along the street. During the next four decades I struggled against my suicidal feelings and homosexual attractions."[12]

Balancing all these ambiguities in his early life was the constant and unambiguous experience of illness and pain. For one thing, he was born with a cleft palate—a hole in the roof of his mouth. Fortunately, his father was in the military at the time and military surgeons were able to correct the problem with an operation that the family almost certainly would not otherwise have been able to afford. It left him, though, with a speech impediment that he was able to overcome only by means of therapy: he produced his sibilants—the "S"—somehow from the sides of his mouth. Given his later career as a speaker and teacher, this was no small issue.

A problem perhaps related to the cleft palate was poorly functioning eustachian tubes. Any upper respiratory ailment like a cold would settle in his ears and produce a ruptured eardrum. It was excruciatingly painful, and many nights Nana would hold him in his

---

11. Quinn, "Chosen Path," 9.
12. Quinn, "Chosen Path," 16.

agony until the crisis passed. Antibiotics were unable to treat the problem because the rupture would take place within three or four hours after the pressure began to build. "Before I was eight," he recalled, "I learned to stop screaming with this pain and held it in as best I could." He continued to experience this Gethsemane several times a year all the way into adulthood. Finally, in 1982, he underwent another surgery which replaced his right eardrum. Although it also ruptured and he was left with a permanent tinnitus in that ear, his hearing remained good.[13]

But that was not the end of his physical struggles. At about age five, he contracted polio. This led to an early religious experience that was highly meaningful for him. He insisted that one "Brother Jackman," an elderly high priest in the ward, give him a priesthood blessing. Jackman prophesied that although Quinn had a fatal form of the disease, he would recover fully. After only a few weeks in the hospital, with spinal taps and hot compresses, Quinn was able to return home. Although he had to go through physical therapy, the experience left him with no disabilities. There were emotional scars, though. Like many small children whose parents divorce, Quinn blamed himself and interpreted the polio as God's punishment. "I spent the rest of my life," he said, "trying to be the perfect son, the righteous Mormon, the good student and the perpetually nice guy in order to earn people's love and respect. I felt there was something wrong deep inside me."[14]

It would be difficult to overestimate the importance of this early realization of the contours of his personality, though this statement of it was formulated later in life with all the advantages of hindsight into what he had become. One doubts, in other words, how complete this realization would have been in the mind of a boy not yet into elementary school. Nevertheless, one can see in it some of the salient characteristics of the adult Michael Quinn: his perfectionism and the talent to bring it about, his unwavering commitment to his Mormon faith that would cause him to identify himself as a "DNA Mormon" even as the Mormon hierarchy was condemning him, and something of the intransigence of personality and self-righteousness

---

13. Quinn, "Chosen Path," 4–5.
14. Quinn, "Chosen Path," 7–8.

that would render him intolerant of criticism, a sometimes ferocious controversialist and the bane of editors who would attempt to suggest any revisions to the text that emerged from his typewriter. On the other hand, his determination "to be the perfect son ... and the perpetually nice guy" bore fruit in his charming, charismatic personality which made him a popular faculty colleague, devoted friend, and award-winning teacher.[15]

In addition to feeling that he had been healed of polio through Brother Jackman's priesthood blessing, Quinn had another experience that caused him to believe God was his special protector. In 1953 his grandparents took him to the Oregon caves in the southern part of the state. As they proceeded through the labyrinth, Quinn became separated from the rest of the group. At one point, the tour guide turned off all the lights so that the group could experience the total darkness that was natural to the interior of the cave. Quinn kept on going, groping his way along in the darkness. Suddenly he heard an audible voice commanding him to stop. He started to continue, but the voice emphatically repeated the command. At that point, the lights came back on, and Quinn saw that he was on the edge of a precipice which certainly would have cost him his life had he continued.[16]

We conclude this early phase of Quinn's life with his entry into Brigham Young University in the fall of 1962. But first we take note of one final ambiguity he faced at that time: his choice of a college major and a career. He had been an excellent student, and with his intelligence and good grades, he could contemplate any major field and career choice with a reasonable chance of success. During the summer between his high school graduation and his entry into BYU, he moved out of his grandparents' home and struck out on his own for the first time. He would never return. His new home was a room in his uncle's house near the Glendale Adventist Hospital where he found training and employment as a nurse's orderly.[17] Quinn enjoyed helping people, and he found hospital work congenial; he

---

15. Lavina Fielding Anderson, "DNA Mormon: D. Michael Quinn," in John Sillito and Susan Staker, eds., *Mormon Mavericks: Essays on Dissenters* (Salt Lake City: Signature Books, 2002), 329–63.

16. Quinn, "Chosen Path," 10–11.

17. Quinn, "Chosen Path," 52.

would work again, later, in the same capacity at LDS Hospital in Salt Lake City—a fateful event, for it was there that he met his future wife. And it was evidently during that early hospital experience that he developed an interest in medicine. Although undergraduates are not expected to declare a major formally until their junior year (and even after that changes in majors are common), Quinn entered BYU as a pre-med major.

Another current flowing through his life would become a distracting competitor for his attention. While still in high school, Quinn's profound Mormon faith and curiosity led him to an intensive study of the Bible, the Mormon scriptures, and other foundational works of the LDS faith. By the time he left high school, he had prepared card indexes of those works, had written individual studies of papal misbehavior in the Catholic Church and similar shortcomings among historic Mormon leaders, a proper names comparison between the Bible and the Book of Mormon, and a meticulous comparison of the text of the 1830 Book of Mormon with later editions.[18] That study was a telling harbinger of the fierce energy that would propel him through a Yale PhD program in three years and gain him a reputation as one of Mormondom's most competent scholars. It also saw the beginning of his affinity for Mormon history's vexingly difficult subjects—subjects that would try the patience of representatives of Mormon orthodoxy and ultimately lead to his expulsion from the faith that had been his grounding bulwark since youth.

---

18. D. Michael Quinn, "On Being a Mormon Historian (and Its Aftermath)," in George D. Smith, ed., *Faithful History: Essays on Writing Mormon History* (Salt Lake City: Signature Books, 1992), 73.

CHAPTER TWO

GERMINATION

Michael Quinn's first eighteen years, from his birth in 1944 to his entry into Brigham Young University in 1962, were largely years of ambiguity. To the trials that all face in coping with childhood and adolescence were added in his case struggles with ethnic, social, and religious identities as well as the potentially transgressive attraction, from his church's perspective, to members of his own sex. Toward the end of that period, he also struggled to choose a college major and a profession.

During the next ten years, through completion of his undergraduate education, a Mormon proselytizing mission, and a hitch in the US army, he continued to wrestle with some of those same childhood ambiguities. But it was during that period that he began to get his feet under him as a maturing adult.

College is famously a time of rapid and profound change, some of it exciting, some of it discomforting, as students are exposed to new ideas and find their old ones challenged. Both of those were Quinn's experience at BYU. For one thing, he flunked out of his pre-med program. A chemistry professor allowed him to withdraw from a course to avoid a failing grade, but he was not so fortunate in algebra, where he earned a D+. That bad grade, he later found, kept him from graduating magna cum laude and forced him to be content with cum laude. Despite the sobering realization that he was not gifted in every academic field, his was still a distinguished record, and he should have been grateful for the lesson learned: his love of helping people through hospital work was not supported by the scientific skill that would sustain him through medical school.[1]

---

1. D. Michael Quinn, "Chosen Path: A Gay Chicano's Odyssey Through Mormon History," 105, unpublished manuscript in my possession.

Fortunately, at about the same time, he discovered an interest and aptitude in literature and philosophy, particularly stream-of-consciousness novels and existentialism. He devoured William Faulkner, Virginia Woolf, and Marcel Proust. In addition, he read Tolstoy, Dostoevsky, and Joyce (*Ulysses*, at least, though he gave up after two failed assaults on *Finnegan's Wake*). For entertainment, he enjoyed J. R. R. Tolkien's medieval fantasies, which in later years he read aloud to his two daughters and then again to his two sons.[2] He graduated, then, with a major in English and a minor in philosophy.[3]

Although this change of majors from the sciences to the humanities took him a step in the direction toward his ultimate career in history, it was already being undermined by a historical hobby. Before he left BYU, he discovered the special collections section in the J. Reuben Clark Jr. Library (later Harold B. Lee Library) and sometimes even cut classes to immerse himself in the original records of Mormon history that he found there in abundance. "Church history was only a hobby," he recalled, "but it was consuming."[4] (Not until he was in the army in the late 1960s did he make the final transition into the field of history.) Although his strong background in the humanities would provide an excellent springboard into history, his lack of formal class work would haunt him. When, in the early 1970s, he applied for the PhD program in history at Yale University, he had not yet completed the master's program at the University of Utah, and he found it difficult to convince Yale that he had the background to succeed in their program.

Even before his entry into BYU, Quinn had begun discovering things about the Mormon past that troubled him. One was the Adam-God doctrine, which had been adumbrated by Joseph Smith but developed and taught repeatedly by Brigham Young. The year before Quinn entered college, LDS Church apostle LeGrand Richards

---

2. Quinn, "Chosen Path," 108–109.

3. Curiously, Quinn's scores on the Graduate Record Examination, which supposedly rank one's overall educational achievement at the end of the undergraduate program, rated him in the bottom one-third in English. His IQ was rated at 125. Quinn, "Chosen Path," 105–106. At the time of this writing, such college aptitude measurements as the SAT and ACT examinations are being seriously questioned; Quinn's later successes in academic pursuits seem to support such skepticism.

4. Peggy Fletcher Stack, "He's Outside the Faith, but the Faith Is Still Inside Him," *Salt Lake Tribune*, Sep. 28, 2013, C2.

visited Quinn's California ward and gave an informal talk. Afterwards, he asked if there were any questions ("a risky invitation when I was around," Quinn slyly observed). When his turn came, Quinn asked, first of all, about the Adam-God doctrine and, second, about plural marriages sanctioned by the church after the 1890 Manifesto had supposedly abandoned the practice. Regarding the first matter, Richards responded, as Quinn later recorded in a memoir, "that he finds it necessary to place many of the statements of Brigham Young and other early church leaders on the shelf until the Lord reveals more." "At age 17," Quinn recalled, "that seemed like an honest and sensible approach to me." Apparently, thirty-three years later, it still seemed "honest and sensible," for Quinn mentions the issue only once and briefly in his massive dissection of the early development of Mormonism.[5] It would be one of the very rare occasions in which Quinn would venture any dissatisfaction with Mormon theology, and it was quickly and easily put to rest.

The other issue, post-Manifesto polygamy, would be a very different matter. Richards's answer to that question was simply that those who had continued to practice "The Principle" after the Manifesto were guilty of the sin of pride. Once again, for the moment it seemed a satisfactory answer, but before his undergraduate career was finished, Quinn would learn that the "official" church historians like B. H. Roberts and Joseph Fielding Smith had falsified history by claiming that the Manifesto had indeed ended the practice. Quinn would then go on to catalog many instances of post-Manifesto plural marriages, many of them performed by the general authorities of the church. That research would eventually bear fruit in an immense 97-page article in *Dialogue: A Journal of Mormon Thought* in April 1985, an article that would prove toxic to his career as a history professor at BYU and become one of the impetuses for his excommunication. If Quinn had little if any trouble with problematic theological issues, post-Manifesto polygamy was only the first of many instances where he would discover, among "official" histories, issues that had been downplayed, ignored, or covered up in a long-term effort to create a

---

5. Quinn, "Background and Development of My 1985 'LDS Church Authority and New Plural Marriages, 1890–1904,'" *Sunstone*, Fall 2015, 5; and *The Mormon Hierarchy: Origins of Power* (Salt Lake City: Signature Books/Smith Research Associates, 1994), 36.

false, sanitized, and faith-promoting image of Mormon history. In his lengthy efforts to correct that false image, Quinn would create some of Mormon historiography's most massive and sophisticated works. Unfortunately, a corollary—but not altogether unanticipated—result of his relentless truth-telling would be the revelation that some of the church hierarchy could seemingly only handle so much truth, and Quinn's professional career and church membership would be casualties.[6]

Quinn's initial awareness of Mormon polygamy—pre-Manifesto—was a positive one. It had existed, in fact, on his mother's side, and he admired his ancestors' dedication and perseverance in what was, in most cases, a difficult way of life. He even had a similar reaction to his early awareness of post-Manifesto polygamy. He acquired that when someone gave him a copy of Samuel Woolley Taylor's *Family Kingdom* (1951), one of the most delightful books ever written about any aspect of fringe Americana. Taylor was one of thirty-six children of John W. Taylor, a former Mormon apostle who had been excommunicated for his dogged adherence to polygamy well after the Manifesto. Subsequent post-Manifesto polygamists came to regard Taylor as an icon and a martyr to "The Principle," which his own father, President John Taylor, successor to Brigham Young, had unflinchingly asserted would never disappear from the earth and would remain an indispensable hallmark of the Mormon faith. *Family Kingdom* is Sam Taylor's loving, semi-fictional biography of his mother, Janet Maria Woolley Taylor ("Nettie"), one of John W. Taylor's six wives who shared with him the ups and downs of a life on the run, both from federal prosecutors and authorities of the Mormon Church. Despite LeGrand Richards's judgment that the Taylors were guilty of pride, Quinn could see in them some of the same dedication to a principle and a difficult way of life as his own ancestors.[7]

---

6. I once asked Quinn if he were not guilty of a certain naiveté when, after publishing all those records of post-Manifesto polygamy and writing articles like "Mormon Women Have Had the Priesthood Since 1843," he then asked, in effect, "Why do they hate me"? "I wasn't naïve," he responded. He knew, in other words, what he was up against and took the calculated risk anyway. Topping, telephone conversation with Quinn, Apr. 28, 2020. The Mormon women article appeared in Maxine Hanks, ed., *Women and Authority: Re-emerging Mormon Feminism* (Salt Lake City: Signature Books, 1992).

7. Quinn, "Background and Development," 7.

So far, so good, but before he left BYU, Quinn would come face to face with his first example of falsified history coming from Mormon officialdom. It happened in 1965, as a result of an encounter with a classmate, Stephen E. Robinson, a descendant of a post-Manifesto polygamous marriage. In a religion class, Robinson's professor had branded all participants in such marriage as adulterers, and Robinson was outraged. "That religion professor was lying!" Robinson yelled to Quinn in a BYU dorm room. "My grandfather was not an adulterer!" Robinson went on to assert that his family had a recommend for the marriage signed by church president Joseph F. Smith, who had both known about and approved the marriage.

Quinn was skeptical but secured the full name of Robinson's grandfather and resolved to check the story out. The next weekend, he took the bus to Salt Lake City and consulted the marriage records in the LDS Genealogical Library, where he ascertained that the grandfather had indeed married two plural wives with full church sanction, had remained president of the church's California mission for twenty years, and had fathered children with all his wives. "That ended my confidence in traditional Mormon historians," Quinn concluded. "This BYU student launched me on a quest to understand post-Manifesto polygamy and every other historical claim about the LDS Church made by anti-Mormons. In the process, I found that traditional Mormon historians were denying the existence of things that even anti-Mormons could demonstrate even from Mormon sources. ... I was determined to ... do what traditional historians had not been doing: acknowledge all the evidence and still come up with an explanation that was both honest and reassuring for believers."[8] Quinn could not have known it at the time, but he had come up with not just a research project, but a career.

At the end of his first year of college, Quinn decided to take a break and, like many other nineteen-year-old Mormon men, accepted a mission call; his was to the British mission. His success as a missionary was a bit ambiguous. Some of his companions liked him; others did not. He was transferred to different cities quite a bit, which could mean, in journalist Peggy Fletcher Stack's interpretation, that

---

8. Quinn, "Background and Development," 7.

he was "the go-to guy for tough assignments in the British Isles." It could equally mean, given his sometimes stubbornness of personality, that he was a handful for mission leaders and that they moved him around, in part, to get him out of their hair. One telling instance illustrates his incompatibility with the other missionaries. Once, while riding in a van with others, he blurted out that the Book of Mormon had only been changed sixteen times since its first appearance in 1830. It was exactly the kind of research that Quinn was already excelling at, but the information was greeted by a stony silence: while Quinn thought it represented a remarkable stability in the text and would thus be faith-encouraging, the other missionaries reacted with a characteristically Mormon fundamentalism, astonished that the text had changed at all.[9]

By far the most important experience on his mission, though, was one that caused the only major faith crisis in his life: it fell to Quinn's group of missionaries to have to deal with the deleterious effects of the so-called "baseball conversions."[10] It was a worldwide phenomenon that took place not only at various places in the United States, but also in the South Sea Islands, the Philippines, and particularly in Britain and France during the late 1950s and early 1960s. The activity was known variously as the "Basketball Program," the "Beach Party Program," and the "Baseball Baptism Program," which church leaders promoted as a "New Era" in missionary work and referred to it as the "Youth Baptism Program." Controversial from the beginning even among top church leadership, the program was the brainchild of Apostle Henry D. Moyle, who became second counselor in the First Presidency in 1959. Moyle almost immediately became notorious for his loose way with the church purse strings, launching a massive deficit spending construction program which cost, in its first six months, $8 million more than the church's income for the year. Realizing that he had to cover the deficit somehow, Moyle linked it to an accelerated missionary program in the hope that massive conversions would lead to massive increases in member tithing.

---

9. Stack, "He's Outside the Faith," C2.

10. The section that follows is based entirely on D. Michael Quinn, "'I-Thou' vs. 'I-It' Conversions: The Mormon 'Baseball Baptism' Era," unpublished manuscript in possession of Signature Books Publishing.

Moyle's initiative was based on an accelerated baptism preparation. Since 1948 the program of new convert baptismal preparation had been based on a course of as many as fifteen "lessons" missionaries presented to prospects, after which they would be invited to accept baptism. That course was altogether too slow to fit Moyle's schedule, so it was replaced by a drastically shortened course of six lessons which the missionaries committed to memory and recited verbatim to prospects, sometimes all at one time. Astonishingly, even that proved sometimes to be too deliberate to suit Moyle: the program's reductio ad absurdum came in 1961 when French missionaries were told that everything a prospect needed to know for baptism could be imparted in three minutes.[11]

The result of all this was that, in Quinn's characterization, "Mormon proselytizing became goal-driven and pressurized upon the church-wide adoption of this teaching method in 1961. ... Goals, quotas, comparative charts and deadlines were among the 'well-known salesmanship techniques' that Henry D. Moyle made part of the LDS church's worldwide missionary work." Nevertheless, despite the increased number of conversions and Moyle's economizing practice of impressing new converts as volunteer laborers on his new construction projects, the church racked up a $32 million deficit for 1962 and a $5 million shortfall during the first two months on 1963. "Mormonism," Quinn observed, "was teetering on the edge of a financial crisis."[12]

The missionary program, in fact, was losing its soul in its headlong pursuit of numbers. In the British mission, conversions soared to 1,100–1,200 per month as missionaries were forced to work from 7:00 a.m. to midnight and cajoled and shamed into ever higher convert numbers. To achieve those numbers, missionaries resorted to outright trickery: boys were recruited for church sports programs into which they were "initiated" by immersion ceremonies which they rarely understood as baptisms. In the American South, boys from interior areas were bused en masse to the gulf for beach parties which included baptisms in the surf. In the most deplorable

---

11. Quinn, "I-Thou," 5, 11.
12. Quinn, "I-Thou," 5–6.

cases, boys were baptized more than once under different names and whole sheaves of baptismal records were simply falsified.

Finally, in 1962 and 1963, church president David O. McKay had heard enough and sent church officials Marion D. Hanks and Mark E. Petersen to the British and French missions, respectively, to end the quota system. In the latter year, Moyle was stripped of his responsibilities for the financial and missionary programs—a demotion that some believe may have led to his death by heart attack that year.

"On the rare occasions," Quinn notes, "when LDS church leaders have acknowledged the abuses of the baseball baptism era, they have blamed the missionaries. After all, weren't those 19-and-20-year-olds the ones who baptized the unprepared, the untaught, the under-aged, the bribed, the deceived, and the exploited? Weren't LDS missionaries the ones who forged baptismal certificates?" "Yes," he concludes, "but that is blaming the victims."[13]

One of the victims was Quinn himself. He arrived in Britain in 1963 just as the baseball baptism program was being terminated, and it fell to his responsibility, with his colleagues at the time, to clean up the mess the program had created. At one point, the local branch to which he was assigned had eight active members with a total of 150 on the membership rolls.[14] His job was to contact those inactive members—members on paper only—to see what their intentions were and to expel (excommunicate) those who had been "kidnapped" into the church and did not wish to become active.

As the faithful Mormon he was, Quinn agonized over those excommunications. Excommunication is a harsh measure—Quinn himself would live to drink that bitter cup—but the LDS Church at the time offered nothing less draconian. To be sure, this is seeing things through Quinn's eyes; surely, many of those wrongly baptized boys would not have taken it hard to learn that they were now expelled from a church they had never intended to join. And some decided that their baptism was what they wanted and became active church members.

But Quinn did take it hard. It was his first direct experience of truly nefarious activities by the very church leaders his grandmother

---

13. Quinn, "I-Thou," 21.
14. Quinn, "I-Thou," 18.

had taught him to revere, and he saw the suffering those activities had caused, not only among the deceived boys but also among the missionaries who had been exploited in pursuit of nothing but a statistic. "I was twenty years old," he lamented, " and excommunicated three times the number of my convert baptisms." (He had baptized four and excommunicated fourteen.) "I nearly resigned as a missionary and left the church myself during those months. ... I was in tears during the last excommunication court I conducted in that branch. ... My atheism lasted only a few weeks during that process but I remember those months in 1964 as the darkest period of my LDS church experience."[15]

The Mormon mission experience is typically a time of maturation for young Latter-day Saint men, coming as it does during a period when young people are struggling to emerge from adolescence to adulthood. But Quinn had passed through a particularly severe tribulation from which most young men are spared, and it left him with some indelible lessons about honesty and spirituality and the purpose of true religion. "Such abuse of religious ordinances," he concluded, occur "whenever leaders or missionaries of any religion regard externals as more important than one's relationship with God. ... All of us can benefit from remembering the example of those Mormon missionaries during the baseball baptism era who quietly maintained the integrity of their relationship with God, despite overwhelming pressures to the contrary, ... [who chose not to] act or speak as if the Gospel of Christ were a commodity, or regard converts as trophies."[16] Quinn could not have known it at the time, but he would eventually find himself in a similar circumstance where he would have to choose the integrity of his relationship with God and his integrity as a scholar "despite overwhelming pressures to the contrary."

Upon completion of his mission, Quinn returned to BYU. The summer before his senior year, he quit his hospital job in Glendale and moved to Salt Lake City to seek employment. He got a job with a construction company building a freeway overpass. The work, which included carrying heavy rolls of steel cable that dug into his shoulders, was both grueling and dangerous, and he wound

---

15. Quinn, "I-Thou," 19.
16. Quinn, "I-Thou," 23–24.

up getting a cut on his leg which led to his termination as a bad insurance risk. He found a position as a guide on Salt Lake City's downtown Temple Square and announcer for the noon organ concerts. He also went to work at LDS Hospital only six weeks before he was due to return to college. It was a fateful event, for there he met Janice Darley, a clerk in a nurses unit. She agreed to marry him after their third date.[17]

Despite his homosexual leanings, Quinn had decided to live strictly by Mormon standards and remain celibate while anticipating a conventional marriage. The darkly handsome Quinn had had no trouble attracting women and had dated extensively before meeting Jan, but she was, by his account, "the first one for whom I felt immediate sexual attraction." A petite and attractive blond, she was a daughter of Mormon Tabernacle organist Roy Darley and a proficient pianist in her own right. Their marriage in 1967 was based on a mutual passion and eventually produced two daughters and two sons. Over time, though, Quinn found it increasingly difficult to suppress his homosexual urges, which became a widening wedge between them. Eventually, "it became evident that the struggle I thought I could endure alone had created a marriage of love, devotion, frustration, pain and increasing despair for us both as well as growing resentment on her part against me. A heavy price to pay," he admitted, "to fulfill a Mormon boy's sense of duty."[18] We will return later to the tensions that drove the couple apart. For some years in the meantime, they were outwardly a model Mormon couple who read the scriptures and prayed daily, dutifully fulfilled church obligations, and pulled together as Quinn served in the military and began his career as a historian. When he told Jan in 1972 that he was gay, the couple made a brave attempt to soldier on: "After the initial shock, Jan was determined that we would work out the situation together with our mutual love, devotion, and religious faith."[19]

As noted, Quinn graduated cum laude from BYU in 1968 with a major in English and a minor in philosophy. For the nation, the

17. Quinn, "Chosen Path," 89–90.
18. Quinn, "Chosen Path," 94–95. Page 118 narrates a passionate encounter in Berchtesgaden, Germany, that led to the conception of their second daughter.
19. Quinn, "Chosen Path," 134.

year 1968 got off to a bad start with the Tet Offensive in Vietnam, which wiped out virtually all the gains the military establishment had been claiming and led to an ever deepening disillusionment about the war. With his graduation, Quinn lost his eligibility for a draft deferment, and even though he was now married, he came into increasing risk of forced military service. He applied to, and was accepted for, graduate work in English at Duke University, but he decided he might as well face the military issue squarely. Quinn had never been a pacifist and recognized the legitimacy of some wars, but although he had been a left-leaning Democrat since the beginning of his political awareness, he objected to the country's deepening involvement in Vietnam under the Democrat Lyndon Johnson. So he did not wish to serve in that particular war. He decided, though—wisely, as it turned out—that perhaps if he enlisted he could exert some kind of control over the nature of his service, especially since his new college degree would likely open up opportunities for him that other inductees would not have.

He enlisted in the army only two weeks after his graduation and was assigned to a military intelligence unit in Germany.[20] One of the benefits of that assignment was German language training at the US Defense Language Institute, where he was immersed in the language for six hours a day over eight months. Quinn loved the German language and acquired at least a modest fluency, even though that fluency proved to be only of limited utility in his scholarly work after his discharge.[21]

For a couple as culturally sophisticated and intellectually alive as the Quinns, the three years (1968–71) that they spent in Germany would have been a period of enrichment, though Quinn never wrote extensively about that aspect of the experience. What he did write about is the career reorientation he decided upon during that time.

20. Quinn, "Chosen Path," 107–108.

21. Even the most amateur psychologist has to see some significance in this yearning to connect with his Mormon mother's Swiss heritage. During a frustrating period on his mission, Quinn had applied, unsuccessfully, for a transfer to a German mission, even though that would have extended his service for additional language training. The significance of this is rendered even more poignant by the fact that when, for several months in 1999, he lived in Mexico and made a half-hearted attempt to master his father's native Spanish, he deemed himself a failure. See Quinn, "Journal/Journey of a Gringo Chicano in Mexico," unpublished manuscript in my possession.

Although his voracious reading continued to explore stream-of-consciousness fiction, it was during his army years that he decided to become a historian; his avocational reading in Mormon history during college would now become a profession, not just a hobby.

In pursuit of that goal, he arranged for Richard L. Anderson, his former bishop in Provo, Utah, and a professor of religion at BYU, to send him reading material in Mormon primary sources: the six-volume *History of the Church*, the twenty-six volumes of the *Journal of Discourses*, and the four volumes of transcripts of the hearings investigating the legitimacy of Reed Smoot's election to the US Senate at the turn of the twentieth century. In addition, he discovered in the army's library in Munich a directory of all manuscript repositories in the United States and Canada. To prepare for his research once he returned home, he wrote letters to every one of them, inquiring as to what Mormon materials they might have. There were over 300 letters.[22]

For Quinn, his study of history would not be just an academic or intellectual pursuit, but a sort of secular mission. While in Munich, he reported, "I asked God to give me access to the documents of the LDS Church that would give understanding of the internal operations of the general authorities and their activities, particularly regarding polygamy." It was a prayer that God would answer much more abundantly than the aspiring historian could ever have dreamed: "Amazingly, that's what happened when I began graduate study in history."[23]

---

22. "A 'Renegade' Historian's Diaries and Memoirs about His Mentor Leonard J. Arrington, 1970–1999," 2, unpublished manuscript in possession of Signature Books Publishing.

23. "A 'Renegade' Historian's Diaries and Memoirs," 129.

CHAPTER THREE

WUNDERKIND

Throughout much of the twentieth century, research in the archives of the Church of Jesus Christ of Latter-day Saints was a difficult task. The problem centered on the person of Apostle Joseph Fielding Smith, who served as official Church Historian and Recorder from 1921 to 1970, at which time he succeeded to the presidency of the church. Smith's attitude toward Mormon history was manifest in his *Essentials in Church History*, published by the church itself in 1922. Generations of Mormon youth gained their knowledge of church history from successive editions of Smith's book, which was used in seminary classes and elsewhere throughout the church's educational programs. In Smith's view, history and apologetics were one and the same: history was a means of demonstrating the truth of the Mormon faith.

Smith, and most other orthodox Mormons, seemed to think that his book was the last word on the subject of past historical events and that anyone who sought to add to or revise it was a potential threat to the faith. If that had been only one historian's attitude, that would have been one thing, but in his role as Church Historian, Smith, and his assistant, A. William Lund, controlled access to the church archives and thus possessed a chokehold on who wrote Mormon history and what they had access to. Their defensive position meant that few people ever gained access to the archives at all, let alone full, unfettered access, and that those select few tended to write the conventional, faith-promoting history.

One of the few Mormon scholars to breach those secure walls was Leonard J. Arrington during the course of his research for

Great Basin Kingdom: An Economic History of the Latter-day Saints, 1830–1900. Arrington's dissertation (later book) became one of the opening salvos in the so-called New Mormon History, which would separate apologetics from history and bring Mormon history into line with objective, professionalized historiography. In his autobiography, Arrington offers an entertaining account of the strategy he used to overcome Smith's and Lund's suspiciousness and gradually insinuate himself into fuller access to the archives. Over several years, beginning with published material, Arrington slowly moved into theses and dissertations, then the "Journal History of the Church" (a massive scrapbook chronicling church history over the years), and then at last into manuscript and archival material only after having established his trustworthiness.[1] It was a long road that few other historians had the patience or diplomacy to navigate, but Arrington was the stalking horse for the new openness and professionalism that would burst forth in the early 1970s.

In January 1970, Apostle Smith became President Smith of the LDS Church. That meant giving up his position as Church Historian, and, as his replacement, he appointed Apostle Howard W. Hunter. While Smith had begun loosening some restrictions to materials, Hunter's policy was to open everything ... *everything*. Before long, historians of all stripes—even non-Mormons—were examining previously restricted files, up to and including the records of the First Presidency. "Every day was like Christmas morning for researchers in LDS history," Quinn remembered.[2] That new openness triggered a pent-up flood that sometimes overwhelmed the available space for researchers: "You took your chances for getting a place, because the place was jammed with people," the researcher remembered. "The historian's office was just *full* of excitement. ... There were so many people coming in to use the historian's office, a brand new world that had not been the case before, that they put desks and chairs out

---

1. Leonard J. Arrington, *Great Basin Kingdom: An Economic History of the Latter-day Saints, 1830–1900* (Cambridge, MA: Harvard University Press, 1958); Leonard J. Arrington, *Adventures of a Church Historian* (Urbana: University of Illinois Press, 1998), 11–18.

2. D. Michael Quinn, "A 'Renegade' Historian's Diaries and Memoirs about His Mentor Leonard J. Arrington," 3, unpublished manuscript in possession of Signature Books Publishing, Salt Lake City.

in the hallways. The fire marshals would never have approved this, but that's how it was operating."[3] One of those historians pressing through the archives doors and frequently winding up in the hall was D. Michael Quinn.

Quinn, freshly discharged from the army, arrived at the University of Utah in spring quarter 1971. Although, as noted, he had been admitted to a doctoral program in English literature at Duke University, he had decided his love for Mormon history was too compelling for him ever to have his heart completely in literature, and to yield instead to what had been, to this point, an avocation. He chose the University of Utah over his alma mater BYU because the standards for admission to its graduate program in history were more lax: the one undergraduate history course he had taken was insufficient for BYU.[4]

Although he enrolled for classes in the spring quarter, he was ineligible for formal admission to the program until fall. Nevertheless, he was assigned a program director: Davis Bitton, a Princeton PhD in French Renaissance history who was also an active Mormon and a Mormon historian. It was a fortunate assignment. Bitton at the time was working on what became one of the fundamental resources for Mormon history, his *Guide to Mormon Diaries and Autobiographies*.[5] Bitton had funding for the project and could hire Quinn as a research assistant. It was Quinn's first job in history and the place where he began to establish himself as a new *wunderkind* in the field. With a blazing typing speed of 100–120 words per minute and a monkish stamina that drove him through long days with no lunch hours, Quinn was turning in to Bitton single-spaced typed diary transcripts of hundreds of pages that would be summarized for entries in Bitton's guide.[6]

An unforeseen result of Quinn's strenuous work ethic and rapid typing speed was that he sometimes outstripped the ability of the archives staff to keep him supplied with materials, which led them

---

3. Gregory Prince, interview with D. Michael Quinn, Dec. 5, 2005, 3, unpublished manuscript in possession of Signature Books Publishing.

4. Prince, interview, 2.

5. Davis Bitton, *Guide to Mormon Diaries and Autobiographies* (Provo, UT: Brigham Young University Press, 1977).

6. Prince, interview, 2, 5; Quinn, "Renegade," 3.

to open up the archives stacks to him as they had not to anyone else. Some of this was a carry-over from the limited access to the archives during the days of Joseph Fielding Smith. With virtually no one using the archives, there had been little emphasis on processing and cataloguing the material for research access.[7] Consequently, the archivists themselves sometimes did not know where materials were, and they eventually invited Quinn back into the stacks to find what he was looking for. While in the stacks, he would run across other materials that he—and perhaps no one else—knew existed, and he would include them in his research.[8]

This is the way things were at the time of Quinn's first meeting with Arrington. Quinn had been slow to get acquainted with the other researchers, and he was naturally shy. Also his work ethic kept him glued to his typewriter instead of indulging in water-cooler small talk. Finally, he was aware that he was being given access to records that no researchers had ever seen and he did not want to broadcast the fact that he was working in sensitive materials. Nevertheless, he did strike up an acquaintance with Richard Bennett, a graduate student from Canada whose more outgoing personality magnetized even the standoffish Quinn.

One day Quinn arrived at the archives a little earlier than usual and happened to be there when the jovial Arrington walked in. "I had thought that Richard Bennett was friendly, but I had no idea what friendly was until I saw Leonard in action, greeting people and all," Quinn recalled. Bennett, who was Arrington's research assistant at the time, introduced the two. It was only a casual encounter, but when lunchtime came around, Arrington offered to take Quinn to lunch with him and Bennett. Quinn demurred, saying that he was not hungry and usually worked through the lunch hour. Arrington insisted, urging Quinn that he wanted to get acquainted with him, so they had what turned out to be a long lunch at the Hotel Utah.

---

7. Jeffrey Ogden Johnson, who went to work in the archives in September 1969 during the last years of Joseph Fielding Smith, was one of the leaders during the 1970s of professionalization of the archival program. His reminiscences, in Ronald O. Barney, "The Professionalization of the Archives of the LDS Church and the State of Utah: A Conversation with Jeffrey O. Johnson," *Mormon Historical Studies* 16 (Spring 2015): 189–203, are an insider's view of that transition.

8. Prince, interview, 5.

While nothing much came of the encounter immediately, it turned out to be the beginning of one of Quinn's most important professional and personal relationships.[9]

In the fall of 1971, Bitton began to run short on funds for his diaries project and found it necessary to terminate Quinn's employment, though Quinn continued as his graduate student. By that time, Arrington's research assistant, Bennett, had left to return to his own graduate studies in Canada and Arrington asked Quinn to take over as Bennett's replacement. Quinn hesitated because of his commitment to Bitton, but in December he approached Arrington about the job offer and was hired.[10]

It was a somewhat different job than the one he had had with Bitton, which was a research position; now, he would be writing as well. In that, Quinn was an unknown quantity, for neither Bitton nor Arrington had thus far seen any of Quinn's narrative prose, and his only qualification as a writer was an English degree from BYU. (Even after a prolific, award-winning career that produced many professional articles and several immense volumes of narrative history, Quinn remained insecure about his literary ability.)[11]

It was Quinn's introduction to what many—particularly those outside the Mormon Church—would regard as the curious literary galaxy of Leonard Arrington. That solar system was created by two complementary forces: Arrington's consuming drive for literary production and his immense generosity toward graduate students and other junior scholars seeking to make their first mark in the world of historical writing. Accordingly, his practice was either to pay people to research and prepare drafts of articles and books that would appear under his name, or to co-author articles whose publication, because of his great reputation, was almost guaranteed and which would give a young scholar perhaps his first appearance in print.

---

9. Prince, interview, 6.

10. Prince, interview, 6.

11. D. Michael Quinn, "Journal/Journey of a Gringo Chicano in Mexico," unpublished manuscript in my possession. On May 29, 1999, Quinn compares his unpublished memoir unfavorably with Christopher Isherwood's memoir partly because of "my weaknesses as a writer," and on June 8, 1999, he blames the poor sales of his *Same-Sex Dynamics Among Nineteenth-century Americans: A Mormon Example* (Urbana: University of Illinois Press, 1996) on the grounds that "in the hands of a better writer, the book would have sold the first printing in the first year or so."

While some of this could appear close to plagiarism, it was not, for Arrington would heavily red-pencil those early drafts and his hand would be apparent in the final version. And he made sure that his ghost writers were well enough paid that they—including Quinn—generally considered it a fair arrangement and were grateful just to have a job writing history. "I didn't mind being a ghost write[r]," Quinn recalled. "As an English major I was aware of the long tradition of ghost writing. So this was no problem for me."[12] Arrington began this practice while he was a professor of economics at Utah State University and continued it through his years as Church Historian and later as director of the Joseph Fielding Smith Institute at BYU. Although most of his articles were written by himself, most of his books were written either entirely by others or with heavy contributions from others in research and writing. While there is, as is well known, a deplorable tradition of graduate professors stealing their students' research and presenting it as their own, Arrington, as pointed out, was not stealing, and those who contributed to his list of publications regarded themselves as part of a sort of co-operative, a ubiquitous characteristic of the Mormon way of life which Arrington himself had set forth in his *Great Basin Kingdom*. If literary co-operatives had never existed before, they were at least fully compatible with the Mormon co-operative tradition.[13]

Quinn joined Arrington's "co-operative" in December 1971 as a part-time research assistant paid by Utah State University where Arrington held his professorship. Quinn was never a USU student and never visited the campus, nor, for the next several months of his employment, did Arrington ever visit him in Salt Lake City, where Quinn lived. Their relationship took place by correspondence (and perhaps rarely by telephone), in which Arrington would make an assignment, then correct the draft Quinn would submit.[14]

It was a time of considerable productivity on Quinn's part, which vindicated Arrington's instinctive faith in his protégé. After the end of the university's fall quarter in December 1971, which would mark

---

12. Prince, interview, 8.
13. This cooperative ethos is discussed in Gary Topping, *Leonard J. Arrington: A Historian's Life* (Norman, OK: Arthur H. Clark Co., 2008), 109–10.
14. Prince, interview, 8.

the end of his employment with Bitton, Quinn promised, "I can work a 40 hour week for you until the beginning of the Winter Quarter. After that, I can work 15–20 hours a week during school sessions and 40 hours a week during quarter breaks and the summer."[15] Graduate students are infamous for promising more than they deliver, and this sounds like a overly ambitious promise given Quinn's primary obligation to complete his course work and write his master's thesis, but Arrington would learn that Quinn was as good as his word.

Their relationship changed in a major way after March 1972 when Arrington was appointed head of the History Division under the newly reorganized Church Historical Department under the direction of Elder Alvin R. Dyer.[16] That appointment, which required Arrington's resignation from USU, came as a shock to Quinn. "There goes my job"! he thought. "I'm going to have to find another job. I've been fired twice in the space of six months." But it was a false alarm because Arrington offered him another part-time job working for him in the new History Division; in fact, Quinn was the first historian hired after Dean Jessee, who was already working for the department. Quinn would continue in that capacity from April 1972 until August 1973, when he left Utah to begin his doctoral work at Yale.[17]

Quinn's description of his productivity during that eighteen-month period is almost unbelievable, and one can easily accept his report that it "astounded" Arrington. Typically, he says, he would meet with Arrington on a Monday and receive a certain assignment, often on a topic about which Quinn knew nothing. For the rest of the week, until Thursday, he would do the research, and then, in a burst of writing, would create his report of perhaps thirty pages with footnotes, which he would turn in on Friday. And this was on

---

15. Quinn to Arrington, Nov. 15, 1971, Leonard James Arrington Papers, Special Collections and Archives, Merrill-Cazier Library, Utah State University, Logan.

16. This reorganization, perhaps the single most important event in the history of Mormon historical writing, is recounted by Arrington himself in chapter 5 of his *Adventures* and is a central focus of Gregory A. Prince, *Leonard Arrington and the Writing of Mormon History* (Salt Lake City: University of Utah Press, 2016), chaps. 10–23. An important insider's memoir is Davis Bitton, "Ten Years in Camelot: A Personal Memoir," *Dialogue: A Journal of Mormon Thought* 16 (Autumn 1983): 9–33.

17. Prince, interview, 8–9.

a part-time work schedule. "I just thought this was what everyone did," Quinn recalled. "But Leonard let me know that this was unusual, and he would praise my turn-around time, how fast I was able to write, and how well I was able to write a first draft."[18]

Nor was Quinn's work for Arrington to be used without attribution, for Arrington, as all good mentors do, helped Quinn break into publication in his own right. Quinn, to be sure, was happy to remain a ghost writer, but Arrington was preparing him for a historical career of his own. As might be expected, some of his early publications were minor efforts that appeared in church organs, like historical guides he wrote for open houses at the Ogden and Provo Mormon temples and an article in *Ensign* magazine on Edward Partridge as the church's first Presiding Bishop in the 1830s. And he co-authored an article with Arrington for an anthology edited by three scholars in the Reorganized Church of Jesus Christ of Latter Day Saints (later Community of Christ). But soon his work was appearing under his own byline in the *Utah Historical Quarterly*, *New York History*, and most impressively in the *Pacific Historical Review*, the journal of the West Coast Branch of the American Historical Association.[19] It was an important beginning for one who had not yet completed a master's degree.

Despite the refreshing openness of the church archives and the professionalization of the staff throughout the Historical Department with its commitment to thoroughness of research and objectivity of interpretation, change comes slowly, and very early there were hints of threats of censorship. In December 1972 church educator Neal A. Maxwell returned to Arrington a draft of an article Quinn had written about Young University (an early Mormon education endeavor in Salt Lake City) in which Quinn had noted a certain conflict between Brigham Young and John Taylor. Maxwell commented obliquely that he guessed Arrington and his staff would know how to handle such difficult matters, and Arrington interpreted it as a veiled threat of censorship. Quinn's heart sank,

---

18. Prince, interview, 12–13.
19. Citations for these and all other Quinn publications are available in "Long Vita-1997-of D. Michael Quinn," unpublished manuscript in possession of Signature Books Publishing.

for he had documented the disagreement closely and thought it was an important issue in the history of the university. After looking it over, Arrington worked out a compromise by softening some of Quinn's language while leaving the substance of his argument intact. But Quinn was alarmed: "This experience caused me to wonder how much difficulty I will have [in] saying what I feel needs to be said in my [MA thesis]."[20]

Quinn's worries only deepened when, on the same occasion, Arrington actually asked to read the thesis, adding that "it might be necessary to ask me to delete some things for the welfare of the [Church Historical] Department. ... Both of us recognize that my thesis could be unpopular with powerful people. I dislike the idea of censorship— even only as a hypothetical possibility—but I guess it is an inescapable thing[,] especially in this business [of Mormon history]."[21]

It was a prescient fear, for the hypothetical became the inescapable when Quinn saw that Arrington had heavily red-penciled a draft of the thesis. A sticking point appeared in a five-page section in which Quinn discussed a little-known practice during the Nauvoo period of Mormon history of theocratic anointing of the Mormon prophet as a king on Earth. Arrington ordered him to remove it (Quinn's language on this is unequivocal), warning him that it was such a sensitive issue that it would cause Quinn to be disbarred from using the church archives and destroy his career. Quinn refused, and insisted on leaving it in. "I had all the quotes and all the citations," he remembered. "It was good stuff, and I didn't want to give it up." A major crisis had emerged between mentor and protégé.[22]

Arrington felt so strongly about the matter that he summoned Quinn to a meeting with him, Davis Bitton, and James B. Allen. (The History Division was organized like a Mormon ward or stake, with a bishop or stake president and two counselors: Bitton and Allen were, as Assistant Historians, Arrington's "counselors.") All had read the passage in question and took turns, in order of seniority, grilling Quinn on the desirability of deleting it. In the end,

---

20. Quinn, "Renegade," Dec. 7, 1972.

21. Quinn, "Renegade," Dec. 7, 1972.

22. Prince, interview, 14–15. Quinn's thesis was "Organizational Development and Social Origins of the Mormon Hierarchy, 1832–1932—A Prosopographical Study," MA thesis, University of Utah, 1973.

Arrington prevailed by casting the issue as a test of their friendship, and Quinn took the passage out.[23] At the time, the episode could have been construed as a dust-up between a stubborn neophyte who lacked the experience to foresee long-term consequences, and three wiser veterans who could. Looking back, though, the episode was fraught with foreshadowings of Quinn's contentious career. It was not the last time his findings would come into conflict with church orthodoxy, nor the last time that his obstinacy would drive decisions not in his own better interests.

So it was during his Bitton–Arrington years at the University of Utah and the History Division that Quinn sent down the first roots of what was to become a remarkable historical career. But he gave as good as he got. His research and writing while on his mentors' payrolls made important contributions to the newly emerging professionalization of Mormon historical writing during the 1970s, and his writings on his own behalf became the harbingers of a productive record of publications. But perhaps the most profound and lasting contribution Quinn made during that time was in the area of archives, not in historical research and publication.

Always scouring in the archives stacks and anywhere else his tireless curiosity led him, Quinn stumbled upon, in the basement of the old Church Administration Building many boxes of Brigham Young papers and other historical materials from the Young era that he and others believed were unknown even to the archivists, and thus, of course, unarranged and uncatalogued. Investigation revealed that the papers had been stored, from the time of the Utah War in 1857–58, in the home of George A. Smith, who had been Church Historian from 1854 to 1871. The Church Administration Building had been completed in 1917, and at that time the materials in Smith's house had apparently been transferred there: "The material for general use," Leonard Arrington reported, "was placed on the

---

23. Prince, interview, 15. Quinn must have derived some grim satisfaction when he published *The Mormon Hierarchy: Origins of Power* (Salt Lake City: Signature Books/ Smith Research Associates, 1994), which includes, not a mere five pages, but two entire chapters (3 and 4) on theocratic kingship as the dominant theme in Mormon politics during the Nauvoo, Illinois, era. By then, the career-jeopardizing warnings of Arrington, Bitton, and Allen had become irrelevant, as Quinn had lost both his academic appointment and his church membership and seemingly had nothing left to risk.

third floor, and documentary material not yet approved for general use was placed in the basement." What the criteria were for each of those categories were unclear, but as that was just on the twilight of the tenure of Joseph Fielding Smith as Church Historian, a certain capriciousness was to have been expected. At any rate, it may have been the single most important archival discovery in Mormon history. "I lost all track of time," Quinn recalled, "while exploring this seemingly unknown section of 47 East South Temple. I spent four hours sampling this candy-store of Mormon historical documents."[24]

In a pardonable mixed metaphor provoked by his excitement, Arrington felt at first like he was in the Garden of Eden, then like Archimedes in his proverbial "Eureka" moment. The collection filled 150 archival boxes and included some 30,000 letters, diaries in Young's hand and others' as well as office journals, speech manuscripts, and other invaluable material. Cataloguing it kept a team of archivists busy until 1977 and resulted in a finding aid of some seventy-seven pages.[25] While much, but not all, of it was outside Quinn's own research interests, it effectively revolutionized the study of Brigham Young and his era; for the first time, historians could begin a substantial appraisal of that pivotal, controversial character. It did not make it into Arrington's autobiography, but he confided to Quinn "that next to his own call as Church Historian and the establishment of his history-writing staff, the discovery of these MSS is the most important development for the history of the Church in a century."[26]

By mid-1972 Arrington was developing ambitious long-term plans for Quinn. One July afternoon he asked Quinn to drive him home after work, and when they stopped outside his house, Arrington told him that he wanted to be able to raise his salary, but the only way he could do that would be to make him an Assistant Church Historian—a position equal to that of Bitton and Allen. Quinn was stunned. Here he was, making a decent salary doing something he really wanted to do and enjoyed and deep into his master's program.

---

24. Quinn, "Renegade," July 11, 1972.
25. Arrington, *Adventures*, 113–14.
26. Quinn, "Renegade," Aug. 1, 1972.

He had no real ambition to do anything other than what he was already doing. But the seed of a larger idea had been sown.[27]

The following October, Arrington arranged for the department to pay Quinn's way to the annual conference of the Western History Association, meeting that year at the Yale University campus in New Haven, Connecticut. "That was the first Ivy League school I had ever been to," Quinn recalled. "I walked around these ivy-covered walls, and that gothic-modern construction of Yale, and I was just drop-jawed the whole time I was there. I went into the Beinecke [Library], and they had a large Mormon exhibit. Everything I saw at Yale, I just fell in love with it." He learned that Arrington was preparing him to apply to the doctoral program in the Yale history department.[28] And he met Howard R. Lamar.

Lamar was a gracious southern gentleman with a warm, outgoing personality much like Arrington, who was one of his friends. After his undergraduate program at Emory University, Lamar completed his graduate work at Yale and joined the history department as a faculty member, an affiliation that lasted the rest of his career. Although a fine scholar in his own right,[29] Lamar also developed a reputation as an editor and teacher: with Ray Allen Billington, he edited a series of monographs on specific western topics—the Billington–Lamar Series—and in 1972 was putting together an immense reference work, *The Reader's Encyclopedia of the American West* (1977) for which Arrington—and Quinn as a ghost writer—was preparing articles on the Mormons and Utah.[30] One could argue, though, that Lamar's greatest contribution to western history was his seminar at Yale, which has produced a galaxy of first-rate scholars: Richard White, William Cronon, John Mack Faragher, Donald Wooster, Patricia

---

27. Quinn, "Renegade," July 28, 1972.

28. Quinn, "Renegade," Oct. 12–16, 1972.

29. His *The Far Southwest, 1846–1912: A Territorial History* (New Haven: Yale University, 1966; 2nd ed., New York: W. W. Norton & Co., 1970) is a classic in western historical literature. For a concise summary of Lamar's career and influence, see David J. Weber, "Preface" to William Cronon, George Miles, and Jay Gitlin, eds., *Under an Open Sky: Rethinking America's Western Past* (New York: W. W. Norton & Co. 1992), ix–xii.

30. A revised and enlarged edition, *The New Encyclopedia of the American West* (1998) is even more immense. Quinn contributed several articles to the revised edition under his own byline.

Nelson Limerick, and others, not the least of whom is D. Michael Quinn, who have revolutionized the field.[31]

Quinn's interest in graduate work at Yale antedated his 1972 visit. As early as September 1971 he was writing to Arrington: "I am anxious to meet Dr. Lamar, as I would like very much to obtain my doctorate at Yale." To the contrary, both Bitton and the University of Utah graduate advisor had advised him to stay away from western history because of "the limited [job] market." The question was becoming an urgent matter: "After a [proselytizing] mission, three years in the military and one major change of majors, I do not feel I can afford to do much fumbling in the dark." Arrington's advice: "As for employment possibilities, my theory is always to do what you think is interesting and sound and then trust that an opportunity will arise. We have to have faith in secular concerns as well as in religious. If we are doing good and useful things, and using good judgment, surely the Lord will bless the outcome."[32]

In what would generally have been a wise decision, Quinn decided to broaden his options by applying, not only to Yale, but to the University of California at Los Angeles as well. Quinn had grown up near the UCLA campus and had visited it many times, and Arrington had advised him that John Caughey's western history seminar at UCLA was producing distinguished graduates.[33] Finally, he applied also to Princeton because of Bitton's recommendation of his alma mater. In the spring of 1973 Quinn received letters from all three: Yale turned him down, Princeton turned him down, and UCLA accepted him. By that time, his attempt at diversification had become futile: "I had become so invested in Yale, particularly after my interview with Howard, that I decided there was no other place on earth I wanted to go besides Yale. So I turned down UCLA."[34]

At this point, Arrington's role became crucial. Although he

---

31. Lamar's students (though not Quinn so much) have largely been responsible for the New Western History school which has transformed western historical studies since the late 1980s. See Patricia Nelson Limerick, Clyde A. Milner, II and Charles E. Rankin, eds., *Trails: Toward New Western History* (Lawrence: University Press of Kansas, 1991).

32. Quinn to Arrington, Sep. 15 and Nov. 8, 1971; Arrington to Quinn, Sep. 21, 1971, Arrington Papers.

33. Quinn to Arrington, Nov. 8, 1971.

34. Prince, interview, 16–17.

assured Quinn of continued employment at the History Division and even collaboration on a book (topic unspecified), he really wanted to get Quinn into Yale. Accordingly, Arrington wrote to someone at Yale—the dean of graduate studies, the head of the history department, or some such person—asking why Quinn, the candidate he had recommended, had been rejected. The answer was actually clear to Quinn himself: in his application he had stated that he could accept admission to Yale only on condition of a full scholarship, and Quinn recognized that he was not as qualified as the other graduate students they were admitting: "They were putting their money where the golden eggs were, and I was not a golden egg in their view" because he had credit for only one undergraduate course in history and, at the time, an uncompleted master's degree.[35]

In a telling tribute to Arrington's status in the historical profession, the dean of the Yale graduate school called him at home on a Saturday and discussed Quinn's case with him for two hours. Despite Arrington's hard negotiations, the best concession he could get was an offer to admit Quinn on a half scholarship.

Could Quinn afford to accept that? His initial reaction was to turn it down. After all, he was getting a master's degree and he already had a job he loved, with possibilities of writing more and more Mormon history and even collaborating on a book with his hero, Arrington. In the end, the tide was turned by his wife, Jan, and by Arrington. In the Quinn marriage, Jan had always been the fiscal conservative, budgeting their limited resources carefully and avoiding unnecessary expenses. In this case, though, she was so excited about his opportunity to do graduate work at Yale that she urged him not to be overly concerned about the thousands of dollars of indebtedness the program would cost and to keep his eye on the opportunities a Yale PhD could open up. For his part, Arrington pointed out that he himself would eventually retire and that church leaders would be looking for a replacement as Church Historian, a position for which a Yale PhD would qualify Quinn, as a master's degree from the University of Utah would not. The possibility

---

35. Prince, interview, 17–18.

stunned Quinn, and Jan and he soon began making plans for the journey to New Haven.[36]

It was quite a trip. When they arrived in New Haven, they were the picture of the impoverished graduate student's family. They— Mike and Jan and their two children at the time—had driven all the way from Salt Lake City in a Volkswagen with no furniture and only as much luggage as one can visualize cramming into the tiny car. Almost of necessity they had made a leisurely journey of it, with short days and many stops, including some where Quinn could do some research, visiting some Mormon history sites, and staying with friends. "Our first few days in New Haven were a bit of a trial," Quinn reported to Leonard Arrington. "Lacking the money to transport our furniture to Connecticut, we had decided to borrow or pick up cheap furniture here. For the first few days we slept on the floors, which was bad enough, but in addition there were cockroaches all over the place. I was awakened once by cockroaches crawling through my hair."[37]

Things quickly got better. An exterminator got rid of the cockroaches, and Howard Lamar, in his warm. welcoming way, was there to support them. He invited them and two of his other students to dinner the first Sunday and even arranged for the Quinns to borrow two folding beds. "We have picked up some other odds and ends of furniture, and now have most of the essentials."[38]

Most importantly, Quinn reported, "I really enjoy Yale. You know how beautiful the campus is. Moreover, the relationship between the students and professors is far more relaxed that I anticipated." Lamar held a regular Monday luncheon for his graduate students, and Sydney E. Ahlstrom, with whom Quinn was studying American religious history, held a regular Thursday seminar where wines and soft drinks were available "so we would have something to drink while we discussed the Puritans." His other professor was J. H. Hexter, with whom he was studying early modern Europe. Quinn gave Lamar a copy of his master's thesis, but had not yet, in the first few weeks, broached the idea of expanding it into a dissertation. And, as

---

36. Prince, interview, 18–19.
37. Quinn to Arrington, Sep. 24, 1973, Arrington Papers.
38. Quinn to Arrington, Sep. 24, 1973.

always, he hit the ground at top speed: "I will have a heavy reading schedule this year, especially since I hope to take the written exam in the unrelated area [Hexter's field] next Spring, in order to qualify for advanced standing. ... I am hoping to receive advanced standing next fall and try for orals the following spring term. Time and circumstances will tell."[39] Time and circumstances did indeed tell, for Quinn was already on his way to one of the fastest PhD programs ever seen.

Quinn was, from the very beginning, a standout even among Lamar's other high-powered graduate students. After seeing Lamar at the annual Western History Association conference in October, Arrington could report to Quinn that "Howard found me to tell me how well you were doing. He said he is very pleased with you as are other members of the staff. He said that your paper in the seminar was the best of the group and that he has had the opportunity of turning a little work your way, which I am sure you appreciate."[40] That "little work" was employment as a grader in Lamar's undergraduate course. He did indeed "appreciate" the work: "Jan is babysitting full-time and will do some typing work at home to supplement our income. Without the VA educational checks we would be penniless. As it is we are living on the edge of our income from all sources."[41]

Whatever the family's straitened financial condition, it did not distract Quinn in a major way from devotion to his academic work. Lamar turned one of his two-hour seminars over to Quinn for a presentation on Mormon history to 1847. Taking off from an observation by David Brion Davis and Mario DePillis that American historians had largely failed to take Mormonism seriously as a religion, Quinn "tried to give equal weight to the development and significance of theology in Mormonism as well as to the historical personalities and developments." He accompanied his presentation with a four-page bibliographic handout.[42]

By the following spring, Quinn had gotten around to broaching the idea with Lamar of extending the prosopographical study of the Mormon hierarchy into a doctoral dissertation. Lamar "not

---

39. Quinn to Arrington, Sep. 24, 1973.
40. Arrington to Quinn, Oct. 15, 1973, Arrington Papers.
41. Quinn to Arrington, Dec. 1, 1973, Arrington Papers.
42. Quinn to Arrington, Dec. 1, 1973.

only approved my proposal, but was downright enthusiastic about it, saying it would be idiotic for me to begin with a new research topic at this stage of my work. His support and enthusiasm really gave me a boost." In addition, his coursework was outstanding. Although Lamar would not give a grade for his two seminars until June, Quinn had received honors grades from both Ahlstrom and Hexter and expected the same from Lamar. "All things being equal, I could take my orals early in 1975."[43]

When Quinn's dissertation was approved and he received his degree in 1976, it was apparently a record for rapid completion of a PhD program in the Yale history department. Not only that, but his dissertation won two university awards for excellence. The *wunderkind* was on the threshold of a stellar career in history. If he could get a job at all.

Things had changed at the LDS Church History Division since 1973 when Quinn had left for Yale, and the confidence with which Arrington had, at least by implication, promised him a job when he returned with his doctorate was now no longer so solid. In fact, the optimism in which the eager young scholars had flocked into the newly created History Division in 1972 was not as bright. It is a complicated story, which Gregory Prince has dissected in perceptive detail: while Arrington had developed support for the history program among the First Presidency, he had not also cultivated such support among the Council of Twelve Apostles, and opposition from several of its more conservative members had been growing. Coupled with that was the anemic support, at best, that Arrington should have been able to count upon from the mid-level administrators in charge of the history program, like Joseph Anderson and especially G. Homer Durham. One of the consequences was a budgetary tightening which made it impossible for Arrington to create a slot to rehire

---

43. Quinn to Arrington, Feb. 2, 1974, Arrington Papers. "Prosopography" is one of the few jargon terms inherent to the field of history. Most famously exemplified by the work of Sir Ronald Syme on the Caesarian party in the Roman Revolution and Sir Lewis Namier on the English parliaments during the time of George III, it is a technique of assembling what one might call "micro-biographies," in which one establishes familial and personal relationships that then can be turned into a political faction or party. Quinn's 1976 Yale dissertation was "The Mormon Hierarchy, 1832–1932: An American Elite," thus bringing the scope of his study in his master's thesis from 1832 to 1932. Quinn's work became the basis for his three-volume study of the Mormon hierarchy.

Quinn without firing his replacement, which he was unwilling to do, and Quinn understood that. Nevertheless, the situation threatened to leave the twenty-nine-year-old Quinn an unemployed PhD with immense indebtedness and a still growing family.[44]

By the mid-1970s the postwar proliferation of history PhDs was already making for a tight job market, so Quinn had every reason for consternation, especially if he wished to stay in Utah. At that juncture, though, in an exceedingly rare development, no fewer than three academic openings in history appeared in Utah: at Utah State University, the University of Utah, and at Brigham Young University. Dean May, who had been working at the History Division, was interested in the one at the University of Utah, having been informed that the BYU job was only temporary, and Quinn deemed that May had better qualifications than he, with a longer string of publications. May took the position.

Quinn applied for the Utah State University position, but held out for the slim possibility suggested by Arrington that he might yet be able to create a new History Division position for him. Fortuitously, one day Quinn ran into Thomas G. Alexander, a BYU historian, at the History Division, and Alexander asked him why he did not apply for the BYU job. Quinn replied that he thought the application deadline had passed. Alexander assured him that it had not and that he should submit his application. Alexander was the chair of the search committee, and three other committee members had been impressed with a presentation Quinn had made at BYU, so Quinn's application went to the top of the pile. No doubt to his immense relief, Quinn was accepted both at USU and BYU and ended up accepting the latter.[45]

In a frustrating moment of bad timing, a week later Arrington called to say that, after all, funding had become available to offer Quinn a position at the History Division. At that point, it would have been ethically difficult for Quinn to back out of the BYU offer and accept Arrington's, though his decision was made easier by the fact that the best salary Arrington could offer was $5,000 less than BYU's. Notwithstanding, the timing was crushing, for Quinn had

44. Prince, *Leonard Arrington*, chaps. 20–23; Prince, interview, 21.
45. Prince, interview, 22; Quinn, "Renegade," 35–36.

lost the job he had craved and been preparing for over some years. When he hung up the telephone, he burst into tears.[46]

But he did have a job. Not only a job, but apparently at least, the opportunity of a lifetime. True, he would not be working for Leonard Arrington, to which he had long aspired. But anyone with a good weather eye could see that a cold front was beginning to blow in over the History Division and that its future was increasingly clouded. BYU, by contrast, was a well-endowed major university with a large, respected history department. Moreover, as an institution of the LDS Church, research and publication in Quinn's chosen field of Mormon history would be encouraged and supported—as it would not be at, say, the University of Utah, which was increasingly priding itself in its secular identity and its separation from Utah's pervasive religious culture. Research was encouraged at BYU by relatively light teaching loads, research grants, and the magnificent holdings at the Special Collections of the Harold B. Lee Library. What more could Quinn have desired?

---

46. Quinn, "Renegade," 37.

CHAPTER FOUR

MORMONISM AND MAGIC

At this point I interrupt the chronological narrative of Quinn's life with four chapters offering a critical consideration of each of the book-length works for which he is best known.

It happens to most of us once in a while: we encounter a new idea, and while it strikes us as interesting, we do not immediately see its utility nor significance. But we file it away in our memory. In time—perhaps after many years—something happens that jars that memory back to the surface, and at last we can see what we could not at first, that the idea is pregnant with possibilities. It was just such an unforeseen sequence of events that led to the writing of, in my opinion, one of the most creative, original, and fundamental works in the literature of Mormon history: D. Michael Quinn's *Early Mormonism and the Magic World View*. Although Quinn's field is Mormon history and the book's focus, as the title indicates, is on that history, in fact, the book struck reverberations that resounded throughout the larger field of general United States and even European history.

That pregnant event, for Quinn, took place on October 21, 1977, when he visited the Salt Lake City home of then-Patriarch to the Church of Jesus Christ of Latter-day Saints, Eldred G. Smith, a descendant of Hyrum Smith and custodian of Smith family papers, including documentation of the family's folk-magical practices. Smith showed Quinn some of those documents, but Quinn was interested in other things and largely missed their significance.

The light bulb switched on, so to speak, in 1985, when documents, particularly the now infamous "Salamander Letter" describing occult phenomena associated with the creation of the

Book of Mormon, were publicized. Although the documents were eventually exposed as the work of forger-bomber Mark Hofmann, they did call attention to occult practices during the early development of Mormonism. Anti-Mormon historians had long gloated over such things and tried to use them to discredit the church. Even loyal Mormon scholars had had to acknowledge the documented dabblings of the Smiths in treasure hunting, as well as, of course, in Smith's own words, in his story of divine visitations, the discovery of sacred golden plates, and their translation from an ancient language by means of "seer stones." Those scholars, though, had tended to downplay such treasure seeking as youthful experimentations almost as one would play with an Ouija board at a party without imputing any seriousness to its revelations, and claimed that the adult Joseph Smith, as prophet of a new religious dispensation, had grown out of such occult practices after they had served the purpose of creating new scripture.

What got Quinn's attention, though, was an October 1985 memorandum by none other than the LDS Church Education System admitting that "Joseph Smith's involvement in treasure seeking and folk magic remain," even though the Hofmann documents were inauthentic. "Ample evidence exists for both of these," the memo concluded, "even without the [Salamander letter]."[1] "Ample evidence"? Quinn's mind must have flashed back to the documents Eldred Smith had shown him and whose significance he had neglected. "Ample evidence" might mean that there were other such documents that historians had overlooked. Here Quinn had an official church document seeming to encourage scholars to dig in and explore a hitherto neglected element in the cultural environment of early Mormonism.

As things turned out, if Quinn did indeed interpret the memo as constituting such encouragement, he over-estimated it. When the first edition of his book on Mormonism and the magic world view appeared in 1987, it created, on the one hand, almost a Quinn cult

---

1. Quinn, *Early Mormonism and the Magic World View* (Salt Lake City: Signature Books, 2nd. ed., 1998), xx–xxi. The story of Quinn's meeting with Patriarch Smith is given on p. xx and on 340n4. In the interest of accessibility, my citations here are all from the second edition. The first edition sold out rapidly and is now a rare book.

among young Mormon historians energized by what they saw as an opening up of their field to a whole range of new sources and interpretive possibilities. On the other hand, it provoked in conservative Mormon circles, particularly within the Foundation for Ancient Research in Mormon Studies (FARMS), headquartered at Quinn's own Brigham Young University, a veritable *blitzkrieg* of outrage and denunciations. Those denunciations attacked the reliability of Quinn's sources, his interpretation of those sources, and, ultimately, his very loyalty to the Mormon faith of his youth. Already in trouble with some members of the BYU administration and members of the Quorum of the Twelve Apostles for previous writings that had appeared disloyal or even heretical, *Early Mormonism and the Magic World View* prompted an avalanche of disapproval that would lead eventually to his resignation from the BYU faculty and ultimately to his excommunication. "Prudence," he observed in the 1998 second edition of the book, "did not preserve my employment, nor did carefully qualified historical scholarship save me from being labeled as an 'apostate' (heretic)."[2]

Even as Quinn encountered opposition within his own church to his elaborate explication of occult elements in its creation and early development, which his critics thought undermined the church's claim to spiritual and intellectual respect, a similar opposition emerged from the other end of the spectrum, among some secular humanists. Quinn's investigations revealed the existence of a vast literature on the history of magic and the occult among various cultures from ancient times. That literature, however, had permeated the literature of what we might call mainstream cultural history only very little because many practitioners in the field typically regarded such things as beneath serious intellectual consideration; in fact, some of them may have regarded atheism as more respectable than religious belief, let alone belief in magic. Secular Mormon historian Newell Bringhurst, for example, while accepting Quinn as "a practicing, believing Latter-day Saint," considered "disconcerting" his "'personal testimony' of belief 'in Gods, angels, spirits, and devils, [who] have communicated with humankind.'"[3] In time, we shall

---

2. Quinn, *Early Mormonism*, xiii.
3. Newell Bringhurst, in *Pacific Historical Review* 58 (Aug. 1989): 379.

have to consider Quinn's felt necessity to declare his own beliefs as a qualification for his scholarly investigations, but I wish at this time only to point out that he was running into headwinds from both the religious and academic establishments.

Quinn was aware of both obstacles. "As a historian of the Mormon past," he asserts in the introduction to the second edition, "I have never accepted … the boundaries of officially approved history. … I also decline to conceal important evidence directly relevant to topics being discussed. Nor do I feel obligated to accommodate the rational limits of secular humanists. I go wherever evidence seems to lead and present it in the best way I can. I've tried to be faithful to evidence and faithful to faith." "I know of no book review," he continues, "that criticizes scholars for their *disbelief* in the occult as preface to studies about magical beliefs and practices. … As long as authors affirm and demonstrate their effort at dispassionate and balanced analysis, most academics are not offended by an admission of agnosticism or atheism. But many academics feel embarrassed for a scholar who even briefly acknowledges belief in the metaphysical."[4] Such a bold manifesto, which could have been embraced by scholars of almost every religious persuasion and scholars and students at almost any religiously affiliated educational institution, should have cleared the ground for fair consideration of his findings. Sadly, it did not.

One of the intellectually most difficult tasks Quinn faced lay right at the foundation of his book, in the matter of defining what he meant by "occult" and "magical" practices and distinguishing them from practices we would regard as "religious," The task is rendered more difficult and yet more urgent by the fact that his thesis, in part, is that the two categories were closely intermingled throughout history, and "science," too, was part of the mix. Albert the Great, for example, a medieval scientist and religious saint, also practiced astrology. Even as late as the seventeenth century, Quinn points out, such founders of modern science as Francis Bacon, John Locke, and Isaac Newton (Newton was also a complicated man of deep religious faith) indulged in occult practices. By the early nineteenth century,

---

4. Quinn, *Early Mormonism*, xi, xii.

Quinn continues, the Reformation and the Enlightenment (including the Scientific Revolution) were moving Protestantism away from the non-biblical "magical" practices of the Roman Catholic Church and science more and more into empiricism. Early Mormonism was slow to embrace these trends: Joseph Smith rebelled against the rationalism of the Protestant clergy and came to see their churches as apostate, continuing all the while occasionally to practice his occult arts, as did many of his early followers. Eventually, though perhaps not as quickly as Mormon scholars like Richard Bushman maintain, Mormonism purged itself of those occult practices. In losing its "magic," Mormon religious scholar Sterling McMurrin lamented (and Quinn would seem to agree), Mormonism lost something vital: magic "adds a little spice to religion."[5]

But the problem of definition remains: how to distinguish magic and the occult from religion? Quinn begins by excluding from magic and the occult those things that are merely manipulation of natural objects, like noted magician Rickey Jay's card tricks, Harry Houdini's escape feats, and David Copperfield's illusionism. Magic, like religion, thus has to be based on supernatural or preternatural forces that are evoked by a practitioner. Within that spectrum, then, he identifies two proposed ways of distinguishing between the two. One holds that the nature of religion is "beseeching and imploring," while magic consists of "coercing or exploiting," that is, religion is based on praying to God for a certain result, while magic entails ordering Nature to deliver up something, as in water witching or treasure seeking. Quinn, following New Testament scholar John Dominic Crossan, rejects that standard of distinction. "Where is the evidence," Crossan asks, "that religious miracle is always the former and magical ritual always the latter?"[6] Moses's parting of the Red Sea, for example, or Jesus' turning the water into wine would seem to be coercion of Nature rather than supplication, though both are generally considered to be religious acts.

"A more useful distinction," Quinn suggests, "is centered in ethics and personal conduct. Religion prescribes ethics of daily conduct

---

5. Quinn, *Early Mormonism,* 11–12, 134–35; Sterling M. McMurrin, in *Utah Historical Quarterly* 56 (Spring 1988): 199.

6. Quinn, *Early Mormonism,* xxvi.

for all its adherents, not simply its officiators. The ethical emphasis of magic tends to be limited to ritual purification necessary for the successful performance of its ceremonies."[7] By this standard, Mormonism clearly qualifies as a religion. The whole burden of Quinn's book, though, is to show that Mormonism evolved *as a religion* out of an environment rife with all manner of occult practices and devices—amulets, seer stones, astrological charts, lamens (documents with occult symbols), divining rods, and the like—that were enthusiastically embraced by Joseph Smith and more than a few of his early associates, and that they continued to play a role in the new religion not only throughout the rest of Smith's life but until late in the nineteenth century, long after the church had removed to Utah. He maintains this thesis not only against his FARMS opponents who, in what he calls their "definitional nihilism," refuse to recognize any of Smith's practices as occult, but also against responsible Mormon scholars (among whom Quinn would not count many of the FARMS people) like Richard L. Bushman and Richard L. Anderson, who see occult practices playing a role for a time, but then quickly disappearing after the founding of the Mormon Church.[8]

Quinn is particularly hard on the FARMS people, who had gone after the first edition of *Early Mormonism* with a ferocity that, in my opinion, sometimes transgressed the bounds of civility. One of them, FARMS's chairperson, admitted that some of the FARMS writers "were born 'with the nastiness gene.'" Eleven years later, Quinn found himself in the enviable position of being able to release a revised and greatly expanded edition of the book and thus presented with the opportunity to answer his critics.[9] By that time (1998) he had little to lose; with his academic affiliation at an end

---

7. Quinn, *Early Mormonism,* xxvi.

8. Quinn, *Early Mormonism,* xxviii, 134–35.

9. The first edition included 313 pages of text, while the second edition had 646 pages, plus thirty-nine pages of prefatory material where much of his critical response can be found (though his footnotes bristle with such responses as well). Second editions are rarely reviewed in scholarly journals, but *Church History* made an exception in this case. Its reviewer, though, makes the astonishing observation that Quinn's "responses are so partisan that one tires quickly of the combative tone," which will be appreciated only by "those who like academic debates." The reviewer apparently accepts the "combative tone" of Quinn's critics, but not his response in kind. Douglas D. Alder, in *Church History* 69 (Mar. 2000): 225–26.

and an excommunication decree from his church, he felt free not only to answer his critics, but also to eliminate certain "subjunctive, qualifiers and qualified qualifiers" that, out of prudence, his original editors had requested, even though "my analysis and views were not so tentative" and to restore instead "the kind of emphasis and confidence I feel the evidence warrants."[10]

Quinn's aggressive responses to his critics are far too numerous even to summarize here. One example will have to suffice. Otherwise highly respected folklorist William A. Wilson from BYU publicly castigated Quinn for, among other things, his employment of various forms of parallelism, assuming, for example, that because Joseph Smith wore a certain amulet, he did so for the same reasons others had worn such amulets since ancient times. Wilson was essentially saying, Quinn retorts, that "one cannot assume that because Joseph Smith put a lock-and-key on his front door he did so for the same reasons that other people in other contexts have put a lock-and-key on their front door."[11]

Nor can one do more than hint at the vast body of evidence Quinn offers of occult influences on Joseph Smith, yet that is where one finds the most original and significant contribution of the book. One of the most curious features of Mormon history is that those outside the Mormon Church sometimes seem to hold Joseph Smith in higher regard than do church members. Essential to the mythology of Mormon origins is the proposition that Smith was an unlettered, untutored farm boy lacking in the imagination and the materials out of which the Book of Mormon could have been fashioned. Therefore creation of the fundamental Mormon scripture had to have been completely an act of revelation, given to Smith by heavenly visitors who guided him to the buried golden plates and the means whereby he could translate them. The charge Quinn levels against his critics could well be applied to the entire conventional interpretation of Mormon origins: "Defending Joseph Smith from any association with magic is [their] primary motivation. ...

---

10. Quinn, *Early Mormonism*, xiii.

11. William A. Wilson, in *Western Historical Quarterly* 20 (Aug. 1989): 342–43; Quinn, *Early Mormonism*, 94. Quinn discusses his use of various types of parallelism on pp. xxxii–xxxiv.

This ignores the explicit enthusiastic embrace of magical practices by Smith and his associates."[12] Quinn himself, as we shall see, emphatically identifies himself as a believer in the supernatural elements in the origins of Mormonism while yet amassing great piles of evidence of the very natural elements in Smith's environment upon which he drew. Largely missing in Quinn's account is an appraisal of Smith's imaginative genius, which non-Mormon and anti-Mormon writers since at least the time of Fawn Brodie have emphasized, painting a picture of a boy possessed of such an immense natural creativity that he would not have needed heavenly visitors, golden plates, seer stones, or any other external resource. Mark Twain, after all, a similarly untutored creative genius, fashioned a similar oeuvre out of the materials in his environment only slightly later than Joseph Smith. But dissecting Smith's imaginative genius is a subject for another book, and Quinn found ample material for his own large volume simply in assembling the vast resources in occult literature and practices upon which Smith drew.

Joseph Smith, then, like Robert Louis Stevenson's cow, was "blown by all the winds that pass/ and wet with all the showers" in his immersion in the folk culture of his environment, which he then fused with his creative imagination, or, if one pleases, divine revelation, in fashioning the new religion of Mormonism.[13] Smith, in Quinn's view, in his continued adherence to and utilization of occult ideas and practices, was by that time fighting a rear-guard action against current cultural trends. The repeated waves of religious revival in the Second Great Awakening, which at that time were washing over the Erie Canal region of upstate New York, swept increasing numbers of converts into established churches. There they encountered opposition to their folk beliefs from their classically educated ministers who regarded such things as naïve superstition. Smith's adherence to those very beliefs led him, in part, to regard those established churches as apostate and to establish his new Mormon church as an alternative to them.[14] What was the reason for Smith's persistence?

---

12. Quinn, *Early Mormonism*, xxviii.

13. Stevenson's rhyme is quoted, most accessibly to most of us, in William Strunk Jr. and E. B. White, *The Elements of Style* (New York: Macmillan Publishing Co., 3rd ed., 1979), 85.

14. Quinn, *Early Mormonism*, 31.

In Quinn's view, Smith had never seen his youthful employment of occult devices in the search for buried treasure as essentially
different from his quest for religious enlightenment: "Magic and
treasure-seeking," Quinn points out, "were an integral part of the
Smith family's religious quest." As time went by, however, Smith's
thinking evolved from regarding such things as divining rods as
ways of seeking treasure and more as ways of seeking information. He became, in Quinn's words, more of a "treasure seer" than
a "treasure digger"; that is, his religious quest gradually supplanted
his quest for wealth. To be sure, "It is an overstatement ... to claim
that Smith as a treasure-seer was not interested in financial gain. ...
Because his family was poor, Joseph, Jr. had both financial and metaphysical interest in the treasure-quest."[15] Nevertheless, "the 1820–30
transformation of Joseph Smith from farm boy to seer was ... [ac-
complished by] the intertwining of what many others separated into
distinct categories of divine and occult, religion and magic."[16]

This shift from treasure-seeker to treasure-seer produced con-
tradictory consequences. On the one hand, many of Smith's early
followers did not share his religious quest, and apostatized from his
new church as he moved away from treasure-seeking. On the other
hand, among others of his followers, his occult practices became an
embarrassment as time passed and the Mormon Church sought to
become a respected part of the spectrum of established Christian
churches. Brigham Young, for example, who is often portrayed (with
good reason) as the rational, hard-fisted church organizer in contrast with Smith as the starry-eyed spiritual seeker, had no interest
in practicing the occult arts as did many other early Mormons who
even followed him to Utah, though he continued to tolerate such
things in the hands of others.[17]

Finally, before we complete our discussion of *Early Mormonism and the Magic World View*, it is worth taking a look at Quinn's
personal relationship to his materials. Early in the second edition,
Quinn asks us to "remember the caution of analytical philosopher
Ludwig Wittgenstein, 'I must not make a case for magic, nor may I

15. Quinn, *Early Mormonism*, 30–31, 34, 65.
16. Quinn, *Early Mormonism*, 175.
17. Quinn, *Early Mormonism*, 246, 250.

make fun of it. The depth of magic should be preserved.'"[18] Surely any fair reading of his book would support the conclusion that Quinn achieves that goal, of preserving the depth of magic and the integrity of the people throughout history, including Joseph Smith, who took seriously the practices of magic and the occult. The modern secular historian, though, is taken aback when Quinn goes beyond the mere quest for an objective relationship with his materials to assert "that when books emphasize peoples' claims for metaphysical reality, there should be a statement about whether the author believes such a dimension does exist or is even possible. ... I see an academic necessity," he continues, "to state one's own frame of reference when writing about the metaphysical."[19] True to form, he then goes on to profess his belief in the truth of Mormonism and his conviction "that persons of faith have no reason to avoid historical inquiry into their religion or the discourage others from such investigations."[20] Such a protestation might have been seen as a practical expedient in 1987 at the time of the book's first edition, when Quinn was forced to defend himself as attacks from FARMS and certain LDS general authorities for whom mention of anything controversial was a threat to faith itself. But these statements come from the second edition of 1998, when "prudence," he observed, "did not preserve my employment, nor did carefully qualified historical scholarship save me from being labeled an apostate (heretic)" and he had been actually excommunicated.[21] By that time, presumably, everything he had to lose had been lost, and one has to interpret this felt necessity of professing his faith as a tenet of philosophy rather than a practical expedient.

The literature of historical methodology is replete with admonitions to approach objectivity as closely as possible, even as it acknowledges that such a thing is theoretically impossible. But memory does not readily dredge up admonitions like Quinn's to declare one's personal opinion about his subject matter. Some historians, of course, work harder and succeed better at achieving objectivity than others: one thinks, for example, of Perry Miller, whose two-volume

---

18. Quinn, *Early Mormonism*, xiii.
19. Quinn, *Early Mormonism*, xii.
20. Quinn, *Early Mormonism*, xxxviii.
21. Quinn, *Early Mormonism*, xiii.

The New England Mind, along with his other books, is the most elaborate explication of American Puritanism ever penned. Miller was an atheist. While Miller's beliefs, or lack of them, are of some interest, an awareness of them does not illuminate his treatment of Puritanism. His books, after all, are about Puritanism, not about Miller, just as Quinn's book is about Joseph Smith and his associates, not about Quinn.

My point is that it should matter not at all if a historian of a religion personally believes in that religion, or if a historian of magic herself believes in magic. What matters is that the historian acknowledge that the *subjects* of his history believed in that religion or that magic and that, as Wittgenstein admonished, she take those beliefs seriously and respectfully and tries to see them from the inside and interpret them fairly. What should matter to Quinn's readers is not that Quinn believes in "Gods, angels, spirits and devils," but rather that Joseph Smith believed in them.

CHAPTER FIVE

THE HIERARCHY SERIES

There is a well-known proverb to the effect that if you ever watch sausage being made, you will not eat that sausage. The meaning, of course, is that while the final product may look appetizing in the butcher's display case, the ingredients and the manufacturing process are less so.

I should like to suggest that something similar might be said of religion: most people like to look at their religion—whatever it might be—as it presently exists and imagine that it came into existence at one time, integrally and immutably, and that the truths it teaches and their institutional expressions have been eternally valid and unchanged. In other words, the sausage was never manufactured; it just came into existence, and any intimation of evolution casts its validity (or palatability, in the case of sausage) into question.

Judaism and Christianity, for example, see themselves as evidence of the more or less relentless unfolding of God's will as chronicled in the Hebrew Bible through the ministrations of the patriarchs and prophets. From the calling of Abraham and his family as a uniquely favored people, through their exodus from Egyptian slavery, the imposition of Mosaic law and conquest of Canaan all the way to (according to Christians) the incarnation of the Son of God, his fulfillment of the law and the prophets and his redemptive sacrifice and resurrection, God's will has been clearly manifested in a great saga of salvation. Most Jews and Christians see this as a fairly simple and straightforward story that they accept and live by.

Scholars, as one might expect, see things as more complicated and ambiguous. Many Catholic scholars, for example, see in the darkened glass of sparse documentation of the first few centuries of the church a halting development of even fundamental matters like papal supremacy, the canon of scripture, clerical celibacy, and the seven sacraments. Similarly, many Jewish archaeologists are coming to a consensus that their excavations corroborate almost none of the ancient stories of the patriarchs, the Exodus, the conquest of Canaan, and the empires of David and Solomon that were, instead, later creations around the turn of the seventh century BCE.[1]

It should not be surprising that Mormonism, with its strong tendency to a literalism akin to Protestant fundamentalism, would react suspiciously to scholars with the temerity to suggest that the stories of Joseph Smith's heavenly visitations, his translation of the Book of Mormon from golden plates, and his restoration of primitive Christian institutions through divine revelation should be approached ast anything other than literal fact. That was the assertion of LDS Church Historian and apostle (and later church president) Joseph Fielding Smith's *Essentials in Church History*, which in 1922 established an orthodox tradition of literalism that educated several generations of Mormon Sunday school and seminary/institute students. When Fawn Brodie's biography of Joseph Smith, *No Man Knows My History,* suggested, then, in 1945, that the Mormon prophet could be interpreted at something more multi-faceted, the uproar it created in conservative Mormon circles was immediate.[2]

In the decades following Brodie, and especially after the opening of the LDS Church archives in the late 1960s/early 1970s and creation of the History Division in 1972, the arc of Mormon historical scholarship moved decisively away from the conservative, literalistic certainties of Joseph Fielding Smith. Instead, it tended toward the professionalism of scholars like Leonard Arrington and D. Michael

---

1. The literature of biblical history and archaeology is, of course, vast and delving into it to any significant degree would carry me far from my narrow goal of explicating D. Michael Quinn's trilogy on the evolution of the Mormon hierarchy. Two fundamental works that bear upon my thesis here, though, are John Henry Cardinal Newman's *An Essay on the Development of Christian Doctrine* (1845 and subsequent editions); and Israel Finkelstein and Neil Asher Silberman, *The Bible Unearthed: Archaeology's New Vision of Ancient Israel and the Origin of its Sacred Texts* (New York: Simon and Schuster, 2001).

2. Joseph Fielding Smith, *Essentials in Church History* (Salt Lake City: Church of Jesus Christ of Latter-day Saints, 1922); Fawn Brodie, *No Man Knows My History: The Life of Joseph Smith, the Mormon Prophet* (New York: Alfred A. Knopf, 1945).

Quinn who were less inclined to defend the truth of the Mormon religion and more interested in the objective truth of its history. Rather than seeing in Mormon history solely the working out of God's will, those scholars emphasized both human agency and the foibles of human nature. While most of the scholars involved in what came to be called the New Mormon History were believing, practicing Mormons, they were much more interested in what Mormons had *done* historically than in defending the truth of the faith. As such, they produced histories that were much more human and complex and thus much more believable to the outside world than the defensive, pietistic views of the kind of history that preceded them.[3]

This new professionalism was not accomplished without some opposition; in fact, as it advanced by degree, so did headwinds from within the upper echelons of the LDS hierarchy. The first book produced by Arrington's History Division, Dean Jessee's *Letters of Brigham Young to His Sons*, met with general approval by the Council of Twelve Apostles, accompanied by a subtle warning from Apostle Boyd K. Packer, who would evolve into one of the church's most implacable critics of objective history. Jessee had not seen fit, for example, to excise passages in Young's letters in which he consoled one of his daughters-in-law who was suffering from depression, nor a passage where he admonished his son Brigham Young Jr. to give up the use of tobacco. In Packer's view, saints were to be portrayed as saints, thus immune to the frailties Young's letters acknowledged. According to Arrington, Packer admonished him that "if we determine that we should continue to publish information like this that itself will be an interesting bit of history, for the brethren who have preceded us were very careful to do just the opposite."[4] It was obviously a veiled threat; Packer's and others' opposition in the future would become much more explicit.

---

3. See D. Michael Quinn, ed., *The New Mormon History: Revisionist Essays on the Past* (Salt Lake City: Signature Books, 1992); and Leonard J. Arrington, *Adventures of a Church Historian* (Urbana: University of Illinois Press, 1998). The history of Mormon historical writing is surveyed in Ronald W. Walker, David J. Whittaker, and James B. Allen, *Mormon History* (Urbana: University of Illinois Press, 2001).

4. Dean C. Jessee, ed., *Letters of Brigham Young to His Sons* (Salt Lake City: Deseret Book Co., 1974); Arrington, *Adventures*, 119. See also Arrington, 145, where he lists criticisms from within the church hierarchy of James B. Allen and Glen M. Leonard, *The Story of the Latter-day Saints* (Salt Lake City: Deseret Book Co., 1976).

As previously seen, Quinn's evolutionary view of Mormon history had drawn a heavy barrage of attacks from within the church establishment—especially the FARMS institute at BYU—when his *Early Mormonism and the Magic World View* had appeared in 1987. In that book, he had demonstrated that the history of Joseph Smith's heavenly visitations and revelations so important to orthodox Mormonism, had, in fact, been mired in a thick environment of occult practices that the modern mind was likely to find less appealing, more laughable and embarrassing. That the church had largely grown out of that, as he also demonstrated, was no consolation to the orthodox mind. At any rate, when the first volume of his magisterial trilogy on the Mormon hierarchy, *Origins of Power*, appeared in 1994, he no longer had any reason to soften his commitment to the evolutionary view it advocated (not that he ever had anyway).

At first glance, Quinn's massive three volumes on the Mormon hierarchy may be intimidating—enough so to scare off some casual readers, who would be inclined to consign the books to the realm of the academic specialist. For those willing to venture as far as the tables of contents, though, the intimidation diminishes considerably, for the books are "Quinn-tessentially" Quinn in format: a text of limited scope that is swamped by hundreds of pages of elaborately bibliographical and polemical endnotes and appendices.[5] That imbalance, in fact, can be comical at times: at a symposium convened to discuss *Origins of Power*, one of the attendees complained of the inconvenience of having the endnotes in a separate section which required that the reader keep one finger in the text and another in the notes, and asked Quinn if he had ever considered using footnotes instead. Quinn replied that he had, but the typesetter in one instance found that one page consisted of a single word of text and the rest a footnote![6]

---

5. Specifically, the first volume, *Origins of Power*, has 264 pages of text and 198 each of endnotes and appendices; the second volume, *Extensions of Power*, has 408 pages of text, 222 of endnotes, and 268 of appendices; the third volume, *Wealth and Corporate Power*, has 144 pages of text, 13 of endnotes, and 381 pages of appendices. All three volumes were undertaken as works for hire for Smith Research Associates, San Francisco, then published by Signature Books.

6. [Martha S. Bradley, ed.,] *Myth Making and Myth Breaking: A Discussion of* Origins of Power *by D. Michael Quinn* (Salt Lake City: B. H. Roberts Society, 1995), 43–44. The questioner was Molly Bennion (25–26). Quinn acknowledges the humor in what other

Further, the reader who soldiers on will find that the text itself is quite negotiable. Quinn often employs a simple format in which he states a thesis at the outset, then supports it with multiple examples. This makes it easy to grasp his meaning even when casually scanning the text. Finally, the appendices often constitute invaluable reference sources in which Quinn distills his years of research into conveniently accessible digests. An example would be his "Selected Chronology of the Church of Jesus Christ of Latter-day Saints, 1830–47," the final of several appendices to *Origins of Power*. Quinn claims that it "may be the single most important component in my study," providing, as it does, "a close analysis of leadership topics ... within other contemporary developments of Mormonism" as well as "a reference to all the major issues" raised in the study, and "a sense for the diversity, the continuities, and the discontinuities of the Mormon experience for both its leadership and its rank-and-file." In fact, he concludes, "the reader may wish to begin with the chronology."[7]

Joseph Smith's initial vision, Quinn begins, "implied no religious mission, no church, no community, and certainly no ecclesiastical hierarchy." The theme, then, of *Origins of Power* is how Smith got from the Book of Mormon to Mormon*ism* and the Mormon Church. As noted, Quinn treats that process as evolutionary, which I liken to sausage making, not something achieved suddenly in one blinding divine revelation. As such, he continues, that "evolution of authority, priesthood, ordained offices and presiding quorums traced in this study is not obvious to those acquainted with official LDS doctrine and history." That evolutionary process was carried out through changes made in officially "published texts of LDS scriptures and church documents. ... These changes retroactively introduced concepts, people, names, and structures which did not exist in the original revelations and historical documents."[8]

Although doctrinal development could be accomplished through

scholars would consider his excessive documentation: "I've become a parody of myself," he confided to his friend Lavina Fielding Anderson. Anderson, "DNA Mormon: D. Michael Quinn," in John Sillito and Susan Staker, eds., *Mormon Mavericks: Essays on Dissenters* (Salt Lake City: Signature Books, 2002), 360.

7. D. Michael Quinn, *The Mormon Hierarchy: Origins of Power* (Salt Lake City: Signature Books/Smith Research Associates, 1994), x. The appendix is on pp. 615–60.

8. Quinn, *Origins of Power*, 3, 5.

alterations and additions to received sacred documents, development of a hierarchical authority was a different problem. "A hierarchy of spiritual authority," Quinn observes, "is impossible if there is unrestricted access to receive and announce God's will." It is an issue, in other words, of containment of charisma, a problem inherent to all new religions. "Before [1835]," Quinn asserts, "the structure [of the LDS Church] was fluid, and public claims to authority in the church were made largely on the basis of religious experience and charisma rather than priestly power through lineage and angelic ministration." Further, such authority in the early church was capricious: "The early history of the First Presidency is inextricably linked to shifting patterns of favor among Smith and his closest associates."[9]

Smith gradually drew ultimate authority exclusively to himself: "Where I am not," Smith stated, "there is no First Presidency over the [Council of the] Twelve." Quinn at this point devotes major attention, as he was not able to in his master's thesis, to the development of theocratic monarchy during the Nauvoo period. There is a major incongruity, Quinn emphasizes, in the fact that during the Age of Andrew Jackson, supposedly the Age of the Common Man, this new religion advocated an enlightened despotism, "a theocratic monarchy of good men who establish God's laws and govern his people." This was a major element in the contrariness, even hostility, that historically has characterized Mormons' relationships with their neighbors: "By obedience to its increasingly centralized hierarchy, this aggressive Mormon community altered—and usually disrupted—the social landscape wherever it established its headquarters."[10] Unfortunately for the stability of the church, Smith was killed before he established a clear chain of succession to that authority, leading to the confusion of the succession crisis that followed his death and with which Quinn ends this volume.

This theocratic development in the Mormon hierarchy was accompanied, in Quinn's narrative, by an increasing tendency toward violence. "Unlike other American denominations," he observes, "'the church militant' was a literal fact in Mormonism, not just a symbolic

---

9. Quinn, *Origins of Power*, 7, 9, 46.
10. Quinn, *Origins of Power*, 161, 80.

slogan."[11] This observation foreshadows Quinn's elaborate treatment in his second volume of violence on the Mormon frontier in Utah. Here, it is confined to such developments as "Zion's Camp," the Mormon army that Smith led into Missouri to defend the Saints there in 1834, the subsequent creation of the infamous Danites by strong-arm men like Sampson Avard and Orrin Porter Rockwell to purge the church of dissenters often by terrorist activities, and the Council of Fifty, Smith's hand-picked shadow government supposedly created to rule the world after Christ's second coming. Although the latter body included three non-Mormon members, Quinn rightly brands their presence as "tokenism," and considers the body an instrument of Smith's theocracy—a characterization supported by the fact that it voted to ordain Smith a king.[12] These were ugly, ominous developments for sure, and it is perhaps no surprise that "some historians have claimed that Joseph Smith and the rest of the First Presidency were unaware of the Danite organization, but documentary evidence," Quinn insists, "shows otherwise."[13]

Underlying these developments was an even more disturbing principle that Quinn calls "theocratic ethics." This is the idea that Mormonism's theological goals take precedence over conventional ethics and can even justify "violation of criminal laws."[14] It is little wonder that, in view of such developments, Mormons' neighbors in Illinois who were gradually becoming outnumbered and only poorly protected by the duly constituted civil institutions came to feel themselves threatened.

Quinn's last three chapters are devoted to what I have identified as a succession crisis after Smith's murder, a crisis created by his inconsistent indications of where the legitimate succession would lie. There were numerous claimants, whose bids for legitimacy Quinn dissects. Perhaps an even more interesting and long-lasting crisis, though, was over what the nature of Mormonism itself was going to be. At issue was what Quinn calls Smith's "secret heritage," a

---

11. Quinn, *Origins of Power*, 85.

12. Quinn, *Origins of Power*, 93ff, 128. An important source, the minutes of Nauvoo's Council of Fifty, was not made available to scholars, including Quinn, until it was published in 2016 by the LDS Church Historian's Press.

13. Quinn, *Origins of Power*, 93.

14. Quinn, *Origins of Power*, 88.

group of practices like plural marriage and the temple endowment ceremony and institutions like the Danites, the existence of which was known only to a small number of Nauvoo Mormons. Should such things become widely known, they would brand Mormonism as an exotic, even occult, organization, thus hampering missionary efforts and hindering the church's acceptance as a respectable expression of American Christianity. "During the last days of his life," Quinn notes, "Smith's words and acts suggested that he was willing to forsake all the secret developments of Nauvoo—polygamy, the endowment ceremony, and the Council of Fifty." Upon his demise, though, the surviving leaders were of a divided mind. His civil widow, Emma Smith, a dogged opponent of polygamy, and Sidney Rigdon took the position that those exotic elements should be abandoned. "Even those devoted to Smith," Quinn observes, "recognized that the secret legacy was radical, dangerous, and revolting to the sensibilities of most people."[15] But Brigham Young, who gained precedence as Smith's successor through exercise of a more explicit type of personal force than Smith had ever possessed, made the decision that the exotic elements would stay. It was one of the most fateful decisions in Mormon history, one that would place Mormonism at odds with mainstream American culture and cause untold conflict and suffering until the 1880s when the church was at last forced to choose between extermination and capitulation. Quinn's next two volumes would document that history.

So how did all this go down with Quinn's readers? Ever hopeful, Quinn assumed that the truth would speak for itself and prevail: "For most Mormons this book should be informative without being disturbing. ... [Despite its revelations] of early Mormonism's theological evolution, retroactive redefinition in sacred texts, internal conflicts among revered leaders, theocratic activities, militancy, alienation of formerly friendly non-Mormons, succession ambiguities, and violence against perceived enemies." Even those outside the church should find it appealing: "I also expect that nonbelievers will discover the fundamental religiosity in the Mormon hierarchy's world view."[16] Indeed, Mormonism's central doctrine of continuing

15. Quinn, *Origins of Power*, 148, 168–69.
16. Quinn, *Origins of Power*, xi.

revelation through a living prophet who uniquely has an ear for God's voice—a doctrine that logically means that Mormonism is whatever the prophet says it is at any given time—should predispose its adherents to an evolutionary view of its history. Mario DePillis, though, an outsider who is well aware of Mormonism's contrary tendency toward a static, fundamentalist view of its history, warned that Quinn "is probably too optimistic on both counts."[17]

It is difficult to know how far Quinn's ideas percolated down into the Mormon world below its population of historical scholars. I speculate that they may not have penetrated far. As noted, the book's massive size of almost 700 pages is intimidating, as was its $30.00 retail price. It did not invite casual reading. Further, conservative orthodox Mormons would have found reason to want to dismiss Quinn as a troublemaker whose work did not need to be taken seriously: he had abandoned his BYU professorship, gotten himself excommunicated, and divorced and come out as gay.

Mormon historical scholars, on the other hand, could not employ any of those excuses; they had to take Quinn seriously, and they did. The general tenor of the book reviews was positive, and seemed more in agreement with Quinn that his findings should not be faith-threatening than with DePillis's warning to the contrary. Picking up on the food metaphor, Mormon sociologist Armand Mauss predicted that while "the diet in Quinn's book is often very spicy and sometimes hard to digest," there is "hope that it will eventually be assimilated into the general Mormon understanding of our own past. We will all be the healthier for it. ... For the overwhelming majority of LDS members," Mauss continues, "nothing in this book will make any difference in their daily lives, in their religious commitments, or still less in their overarching worldview."[18]

The theme of Joseph Smith's post facto alteration of Mormonism's sacred writings, which one might expect to raise the most eyebrows among the orthodox, surprisingly troubled the reviewers not at all. BYU professor of history Marvin S. Hill, for example, considered the phenomenon to be logically consistent with the central Mormon doctrine of continuing revelation through a living prophet. Quinn

17. Mario DePillis, in *Journal of Mormon History* 26 (Fall 2000): 223–27.
18. Bradley, *Myth Making*, 37, 28.

himself, responding to his critics, stuck to his guns on the matter: "I see nothing pernicious. I see nothing underhanded. I see nothing negative in terms of motivation for the changing revelations—the introduction of texts, or ideas, of concepts, into earlier revelations rather than just simply dictating new revelations."[19]

Historian John L. Brooke and polygamy scholar B. Carmon Hardy complained of Quinn's rather thin treatment of the role of polygamy in the creation of and developing opposition to the Mormon hierarchy, and his choice instead to focus on Smith's theocracy.[20] It was a telling omission, given Quinn's intensive study of polygamy, though his interest lay primarily in the practice's continuation after the 1890 Manifesto.

A similar criticism of Quinn for not fully utilizing his own research came from Hill, who was familiar with Quinn's prosopographical master's thesis in which he studied family and other personal relationships among the prominent Mormons who formed the hierarchy. "Too much of what is vital to the study," Hill points out, "is in the appendices, not really integrated. ... There are an awful lot of important people in the back of the book that had key relationships with Joseph Smith that would illustrate how he used power and how they related to power." Quinn "doesn't deal enough with Mormon 'tribalism,'" Hill continues. "New family ties, adoptions into families, are topics that are very important and should have been dealt with more extensively."[21] It is an important criticism, and one that strikes at the heart of Quinn's method in dealing with the development of the hierarchy. This prosopographer, Hill is saying, does not do enough prosopography.

Quinn did not immediately answer the question as to why he did not utilize his graduate research and method more thoroughly in his first volume on the hierarchy, but he did answer the question as well as utilize prosopography in volume two, *Extensions of Power*. In part, literary accessibility was behind his decision. Literary excellence is not a quality frequently found among graduate theses, but it has to be a consideration in a book to be issued by a commercial publisher.

---

19. Bradley, *Myth Making*, 15, 49.

20. Brooke, in *Journal of American History* 82 (Dec. 1995): 1206–1208; and Hardy, in *Pacific Historical Review* 65 (Feb. 1996): 150–51.

21. Bradley, *Myth Making*, 10, 16.

Although Sir Ronald Syme's prosopographical reconstruction of the personal ties that created the Caesarian party during the Roman revolution is readable enough, prosopography is difficult to render palatable to a non-specialist readership.[22] As noted, the imposing size of Quinn's hierarchy books already provide enough intimidation to limit the popular appeal of the volumes, and he may have understood that elaborate genealogical charts and similar sociological data that underlay his research would likely have meant literary death.

Quinn explained this in Chapter 5 of *Extensions of Power*, "Family Relationships," where he offers a digest of his prosopographical work that is simplified and rendered more readable while yet incorporating research carried out after his graduate school days. Referring, for example, to the genealogical chart on page 167, showing the intricate relationships among four families prominent in church leadership, Quinn explains, "Further research identified more interrelationships during that first century [than his thesis had discovered], and the format of the original charts was probably too detailed for general readers."[23]

Even more than that, Quinn answered critics of the first volume who had expressed frustration at his apparent timidity in interpreting his material by placing it in a more general context of comparative studies of "enterprises and cultures." That had never been his goal, Quinn pointed out: "I believe it is necessary to establish the data before seeking larger contexts, and that was an enormous task.… Although there are interpretations and analysis, my study is primarily descriptive. I leave it to others to provide the comparative analysis and new insights."[24]

Whether this is an abdication of Quinn's responsibility as a historian, readers will have to decide; there was certainly ample precedence for this factual fixation in Utah historical literature.[25] What it did establish is that there is no "Quinn thesis," no larger

---

22. Sir Ronald Syme, *The Roman Revolution* (London: Oxford University Press, 1939).

23. Quinn, *The Mormon Hierarchy: Extensions of Power* (Salt Lake City: Signature Books, 1997), 491n15.

24. Quinn, *Extensions of Power*, ix.

25. See Gary Topping, *Utah Historians and the Reconstruction of Western History* (Norman: University of Oklahoma Press, 2003). See especially the discussions of Hubert Howe Bancroft, 15–20, and Dale Morgan, 147–55.

framework into which later scholars could plug their work. Surveying the larger landscape of Mormon historiography in 2001, Ronald Walker, David Whittaker, and James Allen called attention to this fact: although the two volumes (at that time) in the hierarchy "were filled with encyclopedic data that were often new and untraditional. … [and] while clearly aimed at a radical and more human interpretation of the Mormon experience, the two volumes lacked a unifying thesis or method, even on the central question of Mormon elites. Data often went unexplained or without a context."[26]

This lack of a "Quinn thesis" has tended to determine the way in which subsequent scholars have used his books—in limited, piecemeal citations of his research on specific topics rather than under a grand interpretive blanket. An example is John G. Turner's 2012 biography of Brigham Young. Although Young was, of course, a central player in shaping what Quinn calls the "origins of power" in the Mormon hierarchy, Turner cites Quinn's books only twice: once on the "reconstitution" of the First Presidency as Young's power base against the Quorum of the Twelve after the 1844 succession crisis in which he took over church leadership from Joseph Smith; and on his continuance of the Council of Fifty as his shadow government in Utah Territory.[27] In other words, Turner does not see Young in Quinn's books as some kind of paradigm of leadership or any other archetype, but merely as a power player in specific instances. One presumes, given his stated goals, that Quinn was content to have his work used in that way.

Indeed, the almost random organization of *Extensions of Power* seems to encourage such piecemeal utilization. The first two chapters, for example, deal with the issue of containment of charisma: how does one limit the voice of God to only one pair of human ears, yet compel unanimous acceptance of the message by others? It is a congenital problem with new religions: even Jesus had to remind his disciples, who observed someone outside their group casting out

---

26. Walker et al., *Mormon History*, 86. Danny Jorgenson, reviewing volumes one and two together in *Dialogue: A Journal of Mormon Thought* 31 (Winter 1998): 241, professes to see interpretive elements that Quinn does not claim, nor do I.

27. John G. Turner, *Brigham Young: Pioneer Prophet* (Cambridge, MA: Belknap Press of Harvard University Press, 2012), 172–73n70, and 185n20. The second citation is to *Extensions of Power*.

demons, that "Anyone who is not against us is with us." And St. Paul had to rebuke the Corinthian Christians from becoming exclusive disciples of himself or Apollos: "I planted the seed and Apollos watered it, but God made it grow" (Mark 9:38–40; 1 Cor. 3:4, 6). The problem is especially acute with Mormonism, which claims to have a living prophet as its leader, and one easily expects the early leaders Joseph Smith and Brigham Young to have had to face the issue. But what a surprise, then, in Quinn's book to find chapter three devoted to that problematic apostle and president Ezra Taft Benson, who did not become church president until 1985. Thematically, it fits, but its chronology is jarring. Similarly, chapter 5, which, as seen, deals prosopographically with the familial relationships that tied together four prominent families in the early leadership of the church, belongs chronologically in the previous volume. And chapter 6, on the history of church finances, spans the entire period from Joseph Smith into the twenty-first century and impinges in a major way upon the third, and final, volume of the trilogy, *Wealth and Corporate Power*.

Otherwise, the organization is at least roughly chronological, with chapters on Brigham Young's theocratic rule, the culture of violence and shadow governments through which he maintained his power in territorial Utah. The last two chapters deal with the church's political involvements after Young's day, with major focal points on its traumatic adjustments to creation of a two-party system during its "Americanization" transformation during the 1890s in preparation for statehood, and dissenters like B. H. Roberts and Moses Thatcher. The book concludes with a treatment of the church's controversial involvement in the struggle over the Equal Rights Amendment from the 1970s to the 1990s.

There is a smooth transition from *Extensions of Power* to volume three in the hierarchy series, *Wealth and Corporate Power* (2017), largely because the extensive appendices that constitute the bulk of the latter volume were conceived as documentation of chapter 6 of the former, "Church Finances." But when his publisher informed Quinn that the firm publishes books, not appendices, Quinn had to rework some textual matter to turn it into a book. As a result, like a rear-engine automobile, the skimpy 116 pages of text are powered by the 381 pages of appendices that bring up the rear. And those pages cover much of the same ground as the twenty-seven pages of the chapter in the second volume.

Perhaps the governing theme of *Wealth and Corporate Power* is Mormonism's characteristic blurring of the line between sacred and secular, one of the religion's distinctive features in contrast with traditional Christianity. "Mormonism's system of theology refuses to adopt the worldly and sectarian distinctions between secular versus religious, civil versus theocratic, and mundane versus divine," Quinn asserts.[28] Anyone who has done much research in local nineteenth-century LDS congregation minutes knows that one is almost as likely to find discussions of irrigation rights as sermons on religious morality. Yet the hierarchy has always exhibited an ambiguous embrace of business enterprises, which they have often justified insofar as they extend church influence rather than earn a profit. Church businesses like Beneficial Life Insurance, for example, have dragged their feet in releasing financial disclosures, Quinn claims, for fear of accusation that the church was a financial rather than a religious institution. "The difficulty with such denials," he points out, "was that LDS leaders were responding to categories and assumptions of non-Mormons but answering in the categories and assumptions of Mormonism. In LDS terms, the church was not 'a commercial rather than a religious institution,' but was commercial because it was religious. Mormonism's aims were not primarily temporal."[29]

To illustrate this ambiguity, Quinn employs on two different occasions the most telling literary device in any of his writings. During the first third of the twentieth century, at the very moment when the church hierarchy was trying to deny or minimize its business involvements, Quinn postulates a hypothetical young Mormon man named Brown, an "Everyman of the Mormon Cultural Region," he calls him.[30] Quinn then lists an amazing array of Mormon general authority-owned businesses that Brother Brown's family would have

---

28. Quinn, *The Mormon Hierarchy: Wealth and Corporate Power* (Salt Lake City: Signature Books, 2017), 49.

29. Quinn, *Wealth and Corporate Power*, 54.

30. This "Brown" appears in *Extensions of Power*, 215–16, and in *Wealth and Corporate Power*, 63–65. By the time of his second appearance, Quinn was able to expand significantly the number of Mormon-owned firms Brown's family would have been able to patronize.

been able to patronize to support virtually every aspect of their life, from the jeweler who sold Brown his engagement ring to the bank where he negotiated his home loan to the grocery store where he bought his food and the car dealership where he bought his automobile.[31] It would have been, in other words, not only possible but, in fact, easy to live completely within a Mormon economic bubble.

Finally, it should be noted that Quinn dedicated the third volume to the "memory of Leonard J. Arrington, Mormonism's finest historian, my mentor, and a constant friend." (Arrington had died in 1999, eighteen years before the third volume appeared, though he had lived to see the first two volumes.) The dedication, though, is more than just a tribute to the person, perhaps more than any other, who made it possible for Quinn to get his blue-ribbon education and to become a Mormon historian in the first place. Indeed, Quinn regarded the third volume, in part, as appendices not only to his own first two volumes, but also to Arrington's 1958 masterpiece, *Great Basin Kingdom: An Economic History of the Latter-day Saints, 1830–1900*. Quinn identifies two ways in which his book is a follow-up to Arrington's: first, he had discovered many Mormon-owned economic enterprises that Arrington had not mentioned. Second, his approach to economic history had been different from Arrington's, who had "examined economic processes, while I have been interested in the details of business administration and management per my emphasis as a social historian."[32]

Quinn's hierarchy series is susceptible to the criticism that it represents an outmoded, elitist, "Great Man" school of thought. It is true that the weight of historiography during the twentieth century, both in Europe and the United States, gravitated away from biographies of powerful leaders (or oligarchies, in Quinn's case) and toward a history "from the bottom up," focusing on the European peasantry and the American working class, on minorities and women whose voices have

---

31. In his review of *Wealth and Corporate Power*, Samuel D. Brunson challenges Quinn's list of businesses, pointing out, for example, that Brown's wedding ring and Chrysler automobile were not actually manufactured by Mormons. Quinn's point, though, that the products passed from the manufacturers to the consumer through Mormon general authority middlemen, remains intact. Brunson, in *Utah Historical Quarterly* 87 (Summer 2019): 254–55.

32. Quinn, *Wealth and Corporate Power*, 51–52.

rarely been heard.[33] The criticism is at the same time both valid and somewhat irrelevant. Historiography tends to be a bit faddish, and unsophisticated historians sometimes think that each new trend renders previous schools of thought obsolete. In point of fact, all during the twentieth century biographies of powerful leaders continued to be written and will continue to be. After all, the actions of a Napoleon or a Hitler, although they are only individuals, can have immense effects on multitudes of people over whom they have authority.

Quinn, of course, was well aware of that criticism and answered it by asserting that however much we might study the common people, we must at the same time devote careful attention to the hierarchy whose decisions exerted profound and ubiquitous effects on those common people. "The emphasis in the book," he protested, " is on 'headquarters culture'. .... And so since my focus was on the general authorities, I did make a decision not to make more than passing reference to the fact that there was a very lively church life outside church headquarters and in many respects it was a different kind of church life. ... And so I must plead guilty to the claim or to the criticism that the book doesn't do everything that should be done about early Mormonism. No, it doesn't, I couldn't."[34]

One should not ignore the fact, either, that Quinn's historical writing as a whole embraced all levels of society. While the hierarchy series and the J. Reuben Clark biography were focused on the elite, the Mormonism and magic book and the same-sex dynamics study embraced both folk culture and the hitherto ignored penumbra of gay life in the Mormon capital city.

Nevertheless, the hierarchy series, even within its admittedly limited scope, offers an amazingly comprehensive look at Mormon history. Nowhere else has the attempt ever been made, on the scale

---

33. In European history this movement was prominently represented by the so-called *Annales* school, founded in 1929 by Marc Bloch and Lucien Febvre; in the United States by the New Left of the 1960s. See, for the former, Norman Cantor, *Inventing the Middle Ages* (New York: William Morrow & Co., 1991), chap. 4, "The French Jews," esp. 132, 141–48. The manifesto of the American New Left was Barton Bernstein, ed., *Towards a New Past: Dissenting Essays in American History* (New York: Random House/ Vintage Books, 1969). The phrase "from the bottom up" comes from Jesse Lemisch, "The American Resolution Seen from the Bottom Up," 3–45.

34. Bradley, *Myth Making*, 42, 39. Quinn here was defending only his first volume, *Origins of Power*, but it applies to the entire series as well.

to which Quinn aspired, to integrate the "difficult" aspects of the Mormon past—the *post facto* tampering with scriptural writings, the secretive Council of Fifty, the theocracy, the violent tenor of life on the Mormon frontier, the persistence of polygamy after official denials, and the church's vast financial empire—into church history's mainstream narrative. If he ultimately failed to gain universal acceptance of that integration, it is there nevertheless, waiting for the church and its historical community to grow into it.

CHAPTER SIX

ELDER STATESMAN

Few historical monographs ever sell well enough to merit a second, revised edition. Those that do provide a coveted opportunity for the author to correct the errors and make the revisions that seem inevitably to elude the most scrupulous copy editing, to incorporate useful criticisms from the reviews (or to answer the unfair or mistaken ones), to add material uncovered by subsequent research, and to rethink previous interpretations. It was D. Michael Quinn's fortunate lot to have had that opportunity no fewer than two times: both his first book, *J. Reuben Clark: The Church Years* and his *Early Mormonism and the Magic World View* went out of print and were reissued by Signature Books in revised editions.[1] However fortunate the circumstance was for Quinn and his readers, it is equally fortunate for his biographer, for the second editions allow an analysis of Quinn's final thoughts on his subjects.

Although it is not altogether clear why Quinn decided to accept the invitation to undertake the Clark project, it offered attractions that he would have found appealing. For one thing, it was centrally related to his graduate work on the Mormon hierarchy, for Clark had served as counselor to no fewer than three presidents of the Mormon Church: Heber J. Grant (1933–45), George Albert Smith (1945–51), and David O. McKay (1951–61), the longest tenure in the First Presidency in Mormon history. Also, Frank W. Fox, a professor of history at Brigham Young University, had just completed what many

---

1. The Clark biography was first published by Brigham Young University Press in 1983 and reissued by Signature Books in 2002 under the title, *Elder Statesman: A Biography of J. Reuben Clark*; Signature published both editions of *Early Mormonism* under the same title, the first in 1987, the second in 1998.

regarded as the definitive biography of Clark's secular, pre-LDS career as a lawyer and diplomat, which would free Quinn to focus on Clark's church service.[2] Finally, an immense collection of Clark papers had been carefully processed and catalogued and were conveniently accessible in the Harold B. Lee Library at Brigham Young University.

On the other hand, there were factors that were less appealing. One was that this was to be an "official" biography that would have to be approved not only by Clark's three children but also by LDS apostles Thomas S. Monson, Howard W. Hunter, and Marion G. Romney. Although Clark had been a blunt man who held strong and sometimes controversial opinions and was inclined to state them directly, Quinn would be expected to produce a generally positive image of his subject. We have seen elsewhere how Quinn had bristled at Leonard Arrington's attempt to censor his treatment of Joseph Smith's theocracy in his master's thesis; this project would test how much editorial control Quinn was willing to accept. The project would also test Quinn's objectivity as a historian, for many of Clark's political and social ideas were diametrically opposite to Quinn's own. Quinn, who identified himself as "a lifelong Democrat and leftwing liberal," was naturally put off when Clark and his "fellow travelers regarded *liberal* and *intellectual* as labels of dishonor or disrespect." Similarly, he was repelled by Clark's racism, anti-Semitism, and homophobia. There were, fortunately, mitigating factors: as a person of Mexican descent, Quinn appreciated Clark's love for the Mexican people, and as an opponent of the Vietnam war, he lauded Clark's disapproval of what he regarded as US President Franklin D. Roosevelt's administration's rush to intervention during World War II.[3]

In the end, Quinn passed these tests with high marks. He found, in the first instance, ways to soften his presentation of Clark's language to a point acceptable to the family while yet being honest to Clark himself. And Quinn scrupulously kept his own positions out of his treatment of Clark's. When Francis M. Gibbons, longtime secretary to the LDS Church First Presidency and himself author of

---

2. Frank W. Fox, *J. Reuben Clark: The Public Years* (Provo/Salt Lake City: Brigham Young University Press/Deseret Book, 1980). Quinn's assessment of Fox's book as "definitive" is in *Elder Statesman*, xv.

3. Quinn, *Elder Statesman*, x–xi.

several faith-promoting biographies of church presidents, criticized the first edition of the Clark biography for not turning Clark into a similar moral paragon, Quinn bristled: "I did not regard it as the historian's role to tell readers what to think or what value judgments to make. ... I did believe that it is the biographer's role to explain the context and apparent motivations for a person's acts or words. ... I assumed that many readers who had always agreed with [Clark's] views and activities would find in the biography even more reasons for admiring him, while many readers who had disagreed with him would find more reasons for criticism."[4] One could hardly ask for a better example of Quinn practicing his principle of "functional objectivity": the idea that while absolute objectivity may be impossible, what is possible for historians is to be aware of and curtail their own biases enough to be fair to their subject.[5]

Dividing Clark's biography as Fox and Quinn did into two more or less discrete phases, the secular and the ecclesiastical, accurately reflects the facts of Clark's life. For his first sixty years, Clark developed a distinguished career as a lawyer and diplomat outside of Utah and with only nominal church affiliation: he rarely attended church and even briefly flirted with atheism. Then, in 1932, seemingly out of the blue, the new Mormon president, Heber J. Grant, summoned Clark to be his second counselor, a position Clark retained for the next twenty-eight years, through the presidencies of Grant, George Albert Smith, and David O. McKay. It was a more than meteoric rise for one who previously had held no calling in the church above teaching Sunday school.

That abrupt change, in Quinn's view, manifests a uniqueness about Clark's career with deep roots in Mormon culture. The basic framework of Quinn's book is an opposition within the Mormon mind between "Babylon," the corrupt secular culture of the eastern United States, and the restored gospel of Mormonism and its divinely inspired institutions in the "Zion" of the Great Basin. Brigham Young, the resolute Mormon pioneer who embodied this stark dualism, was

---

4. Quinn, *Elder Statesman*, xi–xii. Gibbons's observation that Quinn's book had been a "warts and all" interpretation was not intended as a compliment.

5. D. Michael Quinn, "Editor's Introduction," in Quinn, ed., *The New Mormon History: Revisionist Essays on the Past* (Salt Lake City: Signature Books, 1992), xviii–ix.

still alive when J. Reuben Clark was born in 1871 in the small Mormon town of Grantsville, Utah. Self-sufficiency—ecclesiastically, socially, politically, economically—was Young's goal for his people, and there was a deep-seated suspicion in the Mormon mind toward anyone who would think that Babylon held out anything of value.[6] That was the value system within which the young Joshua Reuben Clark was reared, but against which he would develop his career.

Quinn gives us a young "Reub" Clark who was, as a teenager, "remarkably devout" for a boy that age, dependably attending church even when his family stayed away. And a dreamer: in one of his nicest poetic turns, Quinn imagines the farm boy sleeping on a haystack on hot nights and as he fell asleep "with the feel of hay on his back, he may have wondered about his future and potential as the image of the stars merged with floating thoughts of the next morning's chores."[7]

Clark's greatest passion during those years, though, was for education. Although his father ran a small private elementary school, the boy quickly outstripped what the father could give him, even repeating the eighth grade simply because there was nothing higher. Eventually he wound up at LDS College in Salt Lake City which, despite its name, was basically a high school program. There he exhibited two controlling desires: to get more than an elementary education and "to distinguish himself in a metropolis despite his provincial background." And so he did: there, "the barefoot boy from Grantsville" was the only one in a class of seventy-five to earn a grade of 100 percent in a course.[8]

Most pregnantly for his future, Clark established himself as a protégé of the young (at age twenty-nine) principal of the school, the polymath James E. Talmage. Talmage oversaw the rest of his secondary and undergraduate education at the University of Utah and even performed Clark's temple marriage sealing for time and eternity. He was, indeed, Clark's "first significant exposure to urban gentility."[9] Once infected, Clark had the fever, and before much time had passed, it became clear that Utah could offer no cure.

---

6. Quinn, *Elder Statesman*, 1–2.
7. Quinn, *Elder Statesman*, 5–6.
8. Quinn, *Elder Statesman*, 7–8.
9. Quinn, *Elder Statesman*, 9.

Moreover, Talmage was not finished with him. When Talmage became curator of the new Deseret Museum, he persuaded Clark to become his assistant. That role, as Talmage engineered it with church officials, would take the place of the proselytizing mission expected of young Mormon men Clark's age. In that "redefinition of what constituted service to the church Talmage inadvertently provided the rationale for Clark's future life as a secular Latter-day Saint." Nor was that all. During that time, Talmage was working on his *Articles of Faith*, the first encyclopedic explication of Mormon doctrine based on a series of lectures Talmage had delivered. He employed Clark to type the various drafts as the manuscript went through revision, thus enabling Clark to joke that he himself had "written" the book. The experience was significant for Clark's future, for it "helped define [for Clark] the limits of LDS orthodoxy and [Talmage's] disciple would impose that orthodoxy on church curriculum when he became a member of the First Presidency."[10]

But Babylon beckoned. Clark embarked on a successful teaching career in Heber City, Utah, and later in Salt Lake City, but he already wanted to go to law school, which led him to the conclusion "that he could achieve his ambitions only outside the Great Basin and outside Mormon culture." Although he had been a decent teacher, the experience had not been satisfying; in fact, it had "left him as desolate as the alkaline deserts from which his people had carved out tree-lined oases. Ancient Babylon brought remorse to the captive children of Israel, but Reuben felt like a captive in Utah and yearned for the lush opportunities of America's eastern seaboard."[11] Reading this narrative, one is impressed not only with the aptness and consistency of Quinn's Babylon–Zion metaphor, but also perhaps with the personal overtones of Quinn's own life with its felt necessity to leave Utah to complete his career preparation at Yale.

There is yet another echo of Quinn's experience in his account of Clark's eventual escape from Utah. Quinn, as noted, nearly rejected the opportunity to go to Yale because of its expense, but was finally persuaded by a partial scholarship and his wife's willingness to work to support the family in New Haven and to undertake substantial

10. Quinn, *Elder Statesman*, 9–11.
11. Quinn, *Elder Statesman*, 12–13.

debt through student loans. Clark, for his part (and perhaps with Talmage's suggestion and assistance) conceived the idea of applying for a position as Utah Senator Reed Smoot's personal secretary. The income from that position would not only support him and his wife, but also enable him to enter law school at George Washington University. He had even engineered a letter of endorsement for the idea from church president Joseph F. Smith. But Smoot, for undisclosed reasons, would have nothing of it. Clark "would never forget nor forgive the indifferent coolness with which the senator ignored this church-endorsed application."[12] The experience may have spawned an enduring hostility between the two men, but it was a harbinger of Clark's own eventual aloofness from church participation, like Smoot's, while residing in Babylon. In the end, Clark financed his program at Columbia University's law school, as Quinn had his in the Yale history department, by loans, in Clark's case an interest-free loan from a Salt Lake City friend.

Upon his graduation from law school, Clark embarked upon a career that almost anyone would envy, including service as solicitor general for the US state department, undersecretary of state, and ambassador to Mexico. Even so, it had left Clark's highest ambitions unfulfilled: senator from Utah, US Secretary of State, and a seat on the US Supreme Court.

When Heber J. Grant called Clark to be second counselor in the First Presidency in 1932, he was a unique choice. Not only had he never served the proselytizing mission that was seemingly *de rigeur* for young Mormon men, he had never served in any high church calling; in fact, his only church service had been teaching Sunday school. Although he had scrupulously observed the Word of Wisdom prohibitions against coffee, tobacco, and alcohol during his legal and diplomatic careers (to the frustration of many attendees at his receptions and dinners who expected access to such things as a matter of course), he had neglected the basic observance of regular church attendance. To be sure, the sparse Mormon population in "Babylon" had made for a scarcity of LDS congregations where such services were available, and the official anti-clericalism in Mexico

---

12. Quinn, *Elder Statesman*, 13.

had made church attendance of any kind a risky business, but Clark had not distinguished himself, either, for strenuous efforts to overcome those obstacles. And he himself had at one point veered close to the portals of atheism, though that was probably a private development known only to himself. So while Grant's choice was not exactly the village atheist, neither was he exactly the Apostle Paul.

On the other hand, the positive qualities he brought to the office were equally unique to his deficiencies. For one thing, his law degree set him apart from his colleagues and predecessors in the First Presidency, among whom even a baccalaureate degree was uncommon. And his work ethic also set him apart. Most of his colleagues in the high reaches of the church tended to use researchers to keep them apprised of pertinent issues that would come to their attention. But one of the qualities that had made Clark such an excellent lawyer was his thoroughness and dogged work ethic that drove him to investigate every relevant aspect of those issues. Characteristic of Clark's style was the lengthy memorandum he would prepare for every matter that came before the First Presidency, in which he would examine all the pros and cons and precedents, much as he had prepared legal briefs.[13]

Not surprisingly, given such thorough research and reflection, Clark was known for an inflexibility in advancing his positions. In a lawyer, such an inflexibility would be a virtue, but Clark had also operated in the political realm where compromise is usually necessary. It was a flexibility that he brought to his church service. Well aware of the hierarchical nature of Mormonism, he would without comment or resistance accede to the decision of the president of the church, who was not only the boss, but also Prophet, Seer, and Revelator whom Clark acknowledged had access to divine wisdom that could properly trump Clark's research and logic.[14] The secretary of state or the ambassador to Mexico might have political or diplomatic concerns that would cause them to override Clark; the president of the church had those as well, but also divine mandates that secular officials could not claim.

Clark's willing subordination within the First Presidency went

13. Quinn, *Elder Statesman*, 49–50.
14. Quinn, *Elder Statesman*, 50–53.

far beyond backing down from his own positions in deference to the prophet. During the presidencies of Heber J. Grant and George Albert Smith, Clark found ways to become a "fixer" for incidental problems that were governed by no official protocols. For one thing, he discovered that President Grant was often behind in his correspondence, so the well-organized Clark found ways to divert to himself correspondence on matters that required no official decision that only Grant was authorized to make. Also, he found ways to tighten access to Grant so that the president of the church was not succumbing to his tendency to divert his valuable time to informal chats with old friends who happened to drop in. Similarly, with President Smith, who was in ill health during most of his presidential term, Clark took responsibility for much of his correspondence and limited access from visitors who might tire him unnecessarily. Finally, with both Smith and his successor, David O. McKay, Clark found himself called upon to deal with persons with no official authority who attempted to insinuate themselves—unduly, in Clark's view—into official workings of the First Presidency. One such was Smith's daughter, Emily Smith Stewart, who in Clark's opinion attempted to take advantage of her father's frail condition to deal with matters that were properly his. The frugal Clark clashed with her, for example, over her attempt to install expensive Persian carpets in the Church Office Building, which Clark regarded as an unnecessary extravagance. A much longer lasting vexation for Clark was Clare Middlemiss, McKay's protective personal secretary, who was known to use her formidable power as the keeper of McKay's schedule to restrict access to him by people (like Clark's followers) of whom she did not approve. Clark himself could not easily be denied such ready access, but he felt that Middlemiss was giving unfair influence to people who knew how to take advantage of McKay's well-known susceptibility to flattery.[15]

Perhaps the most valuable part of Quinn's biography is his perceptive dissection of the complicated relationship between Clark and McKay. During their lengthy association in the First Presidency (1934–61), their differing positions developed into two competing

---

15. Quinn, *Elder Statesman*, 78, 116–17, 156–57.

power groups—the Clark men and the McKay men. The divided mind those positions created within the Mormon hierarchy was to dominate much of Mormon history during the twentieth century. The Clark–McKay association, in Quinn's view, was "the longest presidential association in LDS history ... [and] among the most significant [associations] in Mormon history."[16]

Quinn deftly sets this rivalry into context by noting an irony in the similarity of the two men's backgrounds. Among those were their origins in rural Utah and the fact that both had been outsiders to the hierarchy at the time of their elevation to the First Presidency. Much more significant, though, were their differences in temperament and philosophy. As observed by Marion G. Romney, himself a member of a later First Presidency, "McKay was a gentle poet-philosopher whereas Clark was a determined administrator-legalist." In his sermons, Romney continued, Clark "usually cited authorities in the law and political science," while McKay cited European poets, novelists, and philosophers and occasionally included his own poetry. McKay had a charismatic spirituality that valued visions and miracles, while Clark, despite his precocious youthful spirituality, was suspicious of "overly spiritual" people.[17]

Clark always researched his decisions thoroughly and rarely backed down; McKay made decisions impetuously and sometimes changed his mind. Clark was a nationalist, McKay an internationalist.[18] Clark was a pessimist, McKay an optimist. It was, in Quinn's view, such personal and philosophical differences that dominated Mormon administration through much of the twentieth century.

Quinn is at his best when dealing with the various components of Clark's conservatism, which included not only anti-communism but also anti-Semitism and racism which repelled not only Quinn himself but also other liberals and even moderate conservatives. True to the principles he had asserted in rejoinder to Francis Gibbons, Quinn always tried to put Clark's ideas into the context of his time, when ideas that were common might have later become odious to many people.

---

16. Quinn, *Elder Statesman*, 132. The discussion I summarize here appears on pp. 132–38.

17. Quinn, *Elder Statesman*, 132–34.

18. Quinn, *Elder Statesman*, 134.

Anti-communism was a prominent thread in Clark's conservatism, dating from his repugnance to the Bolshevik revolution during the First World War, through his dogged opposition to what he regarded as the collectivist tendencies of Franklin Roosevelt's New Deal and to the alliance with the Soviet Union during World War II and his support of Senator Joseph McCarthy's investigations during the 1940s and 1950s. Clark always saw Communism as a greater threat to America than Nazism, which, with his underlying anti-Semitism and support for the German people's right to self-determination, led him to tepid support for U.S. involvement in World War II. In fact, Clark's 1936 letter, "Warning to Church Members," was, Quinn points out, "the first time the LDS Presidency has officially attacked a legal party [the Communist] in the United States."[19]

Clark's racism was grounded in white Americans' fear of the "New Immigration" of the late nineteenth and early twentieth centuries. Although he eventually overcame his hatred of Mexicans and Japanese, he never shook his anti-Semitism, which was based in part on his realization that Karl Marx and other founders of Communism were Jews. Like 80 percent of Americans in 1945, Quinn asserts, knowledge of the Holocaust did not modify Clark's anti-Semitism, and he never mentioned the Holocaust when discussing World War II. "Although [Clark] was capable of great compassion," Quinn goes on, "... there is no evidence that [he] ever felt compassion for Jews. He never voluntarily supported any humanitarian aid if it included Jewish people."[20]

Similarly, Clark's racist attitudes toward African Americans was deeply rooted in American culture all the way back to the days of slavery, but also in the racism of his own church, which long denied the priesthood and temple blessings to African Americans. While he eventually came around to the idea of desegregation, he doggedly opposed interracial marriage and even insisted that LDS Hospital maintain separate blood banks so that transfusions of black blood would not be given to whites.[21]

Pointing out that Clark spent one-third of his life in the nineteenth

---

19. Quinn, *Elder Statesman,* 258–63.
20. Quinn, *Elder Statesman,* 336, 338–39.
21. Quinn, *Elder Statesman,* 339, 349.

century and two-thirds in the twentieth, Quinn observes that his cultural values "reflected both eras." Nevertheless, he "was clearly a product of the nineteenth century. He alternatively accepted and resisted the twentieth century's changing views of race and ethnicity." He was dragged into the modern world, though, largely through his belief "that the Gospel of Christ must be universal." And in the end, Quinn observes, regardless of what one might admire or deplore about Clark, "His life will remain as an extraordinary example of integrity and loyalty."[22] One could hardly ask for a more perceptive, objective appraisal.

Elder Statesman, then, despite the caustic evaluations, is one of the great Mormon biographies. Quinn admirably exercised his "functional objectivity" in fairly and searchingly presenting positions held by Clark that could not have been more repugnant to Quinn himself. Even more than that, though, Quinn, though his close study of the Mormon hierarchy, brought insights to his examination of Clark's church service that would have been inaccessible to most other historians. The book stands as a worthy companion to his three volumes on the hierarchy. Most valuable, in my opinion, is the intimate look the biography provides into the inner relations among members of the First Presidency. The president and his counselors always try to present an image of unanimity in their decisions—a unanimity that Quinn intricately demonstrates is often anything but the case.

---

22. Quinn, *Elder Statesman*, 360–61, 425, 428.

CHAPTER SEVEN

SAME-SEX DYNAMICS

"Can an excommunicated member of the [LDS] church ... write an unbiased book about church members and church policy"? asked Alfred L. Pace III when D. Michael Quinn's *Same-Sex Dynamics among Nineteenth-Century Americans: A Mormon Example* appeared in 1996.[1] One can only respond to that with another question: Can a tithe-paying, priesthood-holding temple worker write an unbiased book about church members and church policy? The answer to both questions is yes. Historiography offers numerous rebukes to Pace's "it takes one to know one" thesis: Paul Sabatier, a Protestant clergyman, writing the standard biography of St. Francis of Assisi, or, closer to home, Thomas F. O'Dea and Jan Shipps, a Catholic and a Methodist, respectively, writing credible books about Mormonism.[2] Early in their training, college history majors have drilled into them the principle that there is no such thing as absolute objectivity, that everyone is always biased, and that the best one can hope for is to recognize those biases and compensate for them in an attempt to achieve what Quinn himself calls a "functional objectivity."[3]

Quinn, in fact, is quite straightforward in stating his bias, and it is anything but the anti-Mormonism that Pace and, later, another

---

1. Alfred L. Pace III, "Unfair Book Trumpeted," *Salt Lake Tribune*, Apr. 18, 1996; D. Michael Quinn, *Same-Sex Dynamics among Nineteenth-Century Americans: A Mormon Example* (Urbana: University of Illinois Press, 1996).

2. Paul Sabatier, *Life of St. Francis of Assisi* (New York: Charles Scribner's Sons, 1894); Thomas F. O'Dea, *The Mormons* (Chicago: University of Chicago Press, 1957); Jan Shipps, *Mormonism: The Story of a New Religious Tradition* (Urbana: University of Illinois Press, 1985).

3. Quinn, "Editor's Introduction," in *The New Mormon History: Revisionist Essays on the Past* (Salt Lake City: Signature Books, 1992), viii.

critic, Rhett Stephens James, in a lengthier, more intemperate attack, have assumed.[4] Acknowledging that he was indeed excommunicated for alleged apostasy, Quinn protests that he is certainly not, in his own eyes, an apostate. "By heritage (through my mother), I remain a seventh-generation Mormon," he asserts. "And I define myself as a believing Mormon outside the church toward which I feel genuine affection and for which I have fond hopes."[5]

Some of Quinn's Mormon critics may unintentionally express homophobic assumptions that lie at the base of modern Mormonism and other socially conservative Christian faiths: homosexuality is a perversion of nature, and suggesting that someone may be gay is an aspersion on their character. Quinn is at some pains to refute both assumptions: homosexuality is abnormal (that is, not the sexual expression for the majority of people), he asserts, but not unnatural, and its existence has nothing to do with one's character or morality. Further, sexual dynamics exist on a lengthy continuum from exclusively heterosexual to exclusively homosexual with most behavior in the middle of the continuum having nothing to do with genital sex. Finally, he demonstrates that socially acceptable forms of some same-sex behaviors have a history and that such same-sex behaviors as holding hands, kissing on the mouth, and sleeping in the same bed were prevalent and acceptable both among Mormons and in the larger American culture throughout the nineteenth century and indeed well into the twentieth.

Quinn's critics so rushed to expose what they read as an anti-Mormon bias that they ignored what would have been a more apt question: what was Quinn's own sexual orientation and how might it have borne upon his history of same-sex dynamics? Even more oddly, the question may not have occurred to Quinn himself who, as discussed elsewhere, felt an obligation to state his biases forthrightly.[6] True, as

---

4. Rhett Stephens James, "Historian's Portrayal of Early Mormonism Distorted," *Herald Journal*, (Logan, Utah), Mar. 10, 1996.

5. Quinn, *Same-Sex Dynamics*, ix.

6. Quinn, *Early Mormonism and the Magic World View* (Salt Lake City: Signature Books, 2nd ed., 1998), xii. Pace, who seems unaware of Quinn's sexual orientation, does suggest that such a thing might be looked into, but more as a slur on Quinn's character than a serious question about bias: "Why is Michael Quinn so enamored with homosexuality, and what 'yearnings' does he have"?

just noted, he was forthcoming with his feelings about Mormonism and his Mormon heritage, but one looks in vain for a similarly direct statement of his own homosexuality. Only once, during his discussion of the literature on the causes of homosexuality, he notes that he at one time accepted the theory that it grew from dysfunctional relationships with parents "which was the position of every book I had read and was consistent with the family background of the one homosexual I knew well [himself]."[7] Even more telling, perhaps, is his response to Rhett James's protestation that Evan Stephens, an early director of the famous Mormon Tabernacle Choir, had repeatedly expressed a desire to be married and therefore could not have been gay. Irish wit Oscar Wilde, Quinn points out, had been married with two sons during the time he was carrying on a homosexual relationship.[8] Quinn's example is apt, but his own case would have been even more so, for he had been married and fathered four children. Perhaps he thought that by 1996 his status as an openly gay man was widely enough known that he did not need to mention it, but then his loyalty to his church even as an excommunicated Mormon was equally well known, and he felt obligated to restate that.

"I prefer to write about the silences in traditional history," Quinn informs readers at the outset of *Same-Sex Dynamics*.[9] Like magic, which he had written about previously, same-sex dynamics is certainly one of those silences, but Quinn makes it speak eloquently. Careful to avoid claiming too much for his subject, he accepts that perhaps 90 percent of humanity is located within the heterosexual part of the continuum.[10] And one of the most significant—not to say startling—parts of the book (chaps. 2–6) contain his discussion of the many ways in which same-sex dynamics are a part of the lives even of those of women and men with strongly heterosexual orientations. His elaborate terminology for those relationships (perhaps his own neologisms) can be quite bewildering—homosocial,

---

7. Quinn, *Same-Sex Dynamics*, 18.

8. Quinn to the editor, *Herald-Journal*, Mar. 22, 1996, 2, courtesy of Signature Books Publishing, Salt Lake City.

9. Quinn, *Same-Sex Dynamics*, ix.

10. Quinn, *Same-Sex Dynamics*, 4. A less cautious writer might have regarded this as a "soft" statistic, for our increasingly gay-accepting culture seems to be turning up ever greater numbers of people recognizing their homosexuality.

homopastoral, homotactile, homoemotional, homoromantic, etc.—
and "on first encounter," as reviewer Stephen J. Stein observes, they
"seem forced and artificial, but they wear well and serve usefully
throughout his analysis."[11]

To most Mormon readers, though, the most controversial part
of the book may be Chapter 8, "The Coming Out of Three Prominent Mormons in 1919," in which Quinn presents evidence for the
likelihood of homosexuality on the part of Evan Stephens as well as
two successive general presidents of the church's children-oriented
Primary Association, Louie B. Felt and May Anderson. It is all too
easy to misunderstand what Quinn is claiming here, as his more
vocal critics seem to have done. He never says he can *prove* the existence of homoerotic behavior in any of the three. Such a thing, in
fact, is difficult to impossible to prove, and can be done only when
a couple is caught in the act or speak explicitly about their intimate
sex life, neither of which is the case here. What hc is claiming—and
this is a central thesis of the book—is that nineteenth-century people (including Mormons) were much more open in expressing deep
feelings for one another, both verbally and tactilely, than became the
case in the next century. That openness makes it easier for the historian to detect homosexuality during that period than later. The fact
that this includes people in high, respected positions in the Mormon
Church should not be unexpected, for they are human beings first of
all and thus susceptible to the same incidence of homosexuality as
the rest of humanity.

It is unfortunate that some readers' outrage at Quinn's "outing" of
three prominent early twentieth-century Mormons in chapter 8 has
seemed to distract their attention from chapter 7, which one might
easily consider the most striking, significant chapter. Called "The
Earliest Community Study of Lesbians and Gay Men in America:
Salt Lake City," the chapter is a dissection of a remarkable study
compiled between 1916 and 1938 by lesbian sociologist Mildred J.
Berryman.[12] Begun while Berryman was a student at Westminster
College in Salt Lake City, it is a collection of thirty-three case studies

---

11. Stephen J. Stein, review in *Church History* 67 (June 1998): 421.
12. Mildred J. Berryman, "The Psychological Phenomena of the Homosexual," unpublished manuscript in the June Mazer Lesbian Collection, West Hollywood, California.

of some 100 gays and lesbians Berryman claims to have known in that city. The document is remarkable, as Quinn points out, because Berryman's subjects "were urban homosexuals" from Salt Lake City, whose "culture and social life reflected America's heartland, rather than the bohemian enclaves and migrant anonymity of New York City or San Francisco."[13] If such a community could exist in Salt Lake City, it could exist anywhere.

As fortunate as social historians are to have such a document, it seems ungrateful to complain about its shortcomings, for it is far from being as useful as it might have been. For one thing, Berryman was anything but an objective social scientist, and her study is marred in several ways by her biases. To have completed profiles of only one-third of the subjects within her acquaintance means that the sample limits the validity of any generalizations the scholar would like to propose. Further, the sample is skewed toward lesbians: gay men comprise only nine members out of thirty-three (27 percent). Finally, Berryman makes virtually no attempt to keep her personal likes and dislikes out of her interpretation of her data: she is judgmental about her subjects' behavior, she obviously disliked men, and she preferred masculine, as against effeminate, behavior in both females and males.

Berryman also erected deliberate barriers to any study of homosexuality among Mormons. Desiring to protect the identity of her subjects (to whom she gives only case numbers rather than names), she was at some pains to avoid naming the city of her study and the religion of her subjects. "Typical of many sociologists," Quinn observes, "Berryman implied national applicability of her findings by not identifying the location of the fieldwork."[14] In fact, she made a feeble attempt to hint that her fieldwork was accomplished in Seattle rather than Salt Lake City.[15] And in her discussion of her subjects' religious background, she avoided naming actual denominations.

Quinn, then, had his work cut out in trying to use Berryman's

---

13. Quinn, *Same-Sex Dynamics*, 196.

14. Quinn, *Same-Sex Dynamics*, 199.

15. In footnotes 5 and 6, pp. 223–25, Quinn discusses his divergent interpretation of both the chronology and location of Berryman's study from the pioneering analysis of her work by Vern and Bonnie Bullough in their "Lesbianism in the 1920s and 1930s: A Newfound Study," *Signs: Journal of Women in Culture and Society* 2 (Summer 1977): 896–97.

study, but in a deft exercise of historical interpretive skill, he was actually able to extract from her the very information she had tried to obscure. For one thing, he established, through college enrollment records, that she had conducted the study in Salt Lake City rather than Seattle. And he was able to "decode" references to her subjects' Mormon background in such terms as "fine old pioneer stock," ("a common phrase among Utah Mormons"), occasional references to a background in polygamy, serving an LDS proselytizing mission, and references to their common use of tobacco and alcohol as rebellion against their own received cultural values.[16] As a result of that detective work, Quinn was able to conclude that "like Mildred Berryman herself, many (possibly all) the persons in her study were of Mormon background."[17] It is Quinn at his analytical best.

"Berryman's study," Quinn concludes, "gives an unparalleled insight into the self-concepts of a sexual minority that was otherwise hidden from the late nineteenth-century and early twentieth-century history of America." The fact that the subjects of her study "lived in a small city that had more in common with the values of America's heartland than a metropolis like New York City ... demonstrates that even in such environments, lesbians and gays of that era had both self-identity and community identity as a sexual minority." And in an even larger sense, "for lesbians and gay men today, this early study provides an opportunity to compare and contrast their own experiences of gay men and lesbians in America's heartland four generations ago."[18]

Why is that not the end of the story? How did that happy circumstance in which gay and lesbian Mormons enjoyed such a strong individual and community identity and expressed their sexual identity more or less openly and with more or less impunity come to an end? Quinn's book cites many instances of tolerance and even encouragement of such behavior during the nineteenth century even at the highest levels of Mormonism. During a time when Mormonism existed in such a cross-grained relationship in so many ways with mainstream American society and culture, there was harmony

---

16. Quinn, *Same-Sex Dynamics*, 197–200.
17. Quinn, *Same-Sex Dynamics*, 197.
18. Quinn, *Same-Sex Dynamics*, 222–23.

in at least that one aspect, toleration for open homosexual expression and activity. And Berryman's research indicated that that ostensibly happy circumstance continued well into the twentieth century. Nevertheless, by the time Quinn was writing his book in the final decade of the twentieth century and attempting himself to live as an openly gay Mormon man, a profound homophobia had descended upon Mormonism, a homophobia that had been dominant within that culture for almost a half century. What had happened?

Almost like Shakespeare's Prospero giving up his magical powers in the last act of *The Tempest*, the similarly magical interpretive powers that had sustained Quinn throughout his historical career seems to have let him down in the last chapter of his last book. (At least Prospero gave his power up willingly; in my opinion, Quinn's just failed.) The shift from toleration to homophobia, he claims, was simply a mysterious change in *zeitgeist* within the Mormon leadership. As those leaders who had come of age in the tolerant nineteenth century passed from the scene, they were replaced by those who grew up in the intolerant twentieth. Even more curiously, Quinn claims that this sea change happened almost suddenly, in the *annus horribilis* 1958, symbolized by the appearance that year of Bruce R. McConkie's controversial, racist, and homophobic *Mormon Doctrine*. Although, as Quinn notes, McConkie could find no earlier Mormon authority to cite in support of his own homophobia, McConkie lumps homosexuality with adultery and other sexual sins prohibited in the book of Leviticus and reckons as a moral failing modern society's spinelessness in shrinking from punishing such behaviors with death.[19]

One lays Quinn's book down with a feeling of having been let down at the end, that such an accomplished historian as Quinn should have been able to adduce a complex matrix of cultural elements that went into the creation of this changed *zeitgeist*. Even an ardent Quinn admirer has a hard time disagreeing with reviewer Benson Tong that "this simplistic explanation would leave almost any informed reader unsatisfied."[20]

---

19. Quinn, *Same-Sex Dynamics*, 375–76.
20. Tong, review in *Western Historical Quarterly* 28 (Autumn 1997): 409.

CHAPTER EIGHT

THE ROAD TO EXILE

Most historians are academics, which means that they live relatively private, obscure lives. They teach their classes, they write their books and articles, they attend conventions, and what little fame—or notoriety—they achieve is usually confined to a small circle of peers and students. When D. Michael Quinn joined the history faculty at Brigham Young University in 1976, there was little indication that his career would be any departure from that norm. What transpired, though, more closely resembled the career of another obscure professor, Martin Luther. As interpreted by the French historian Lucien Febvre, Luther's career was unremarkable in every way until the appearance in 1517 of his so-called "Ninety-five Theses," at which time his fame—or notoriety—shot up to international prominence like a signal flare in the night until his excommunication from the Catholic Church in 1520, after which he returned to obscurity for the rest of his life. Before long, Luther had become relatively unimportant even within the movement he had inaugurated, the Protestant Reformation, while others like Jean Calvin surged to the forefront.[1]

Quinn's beginnings at BYU were probably much like Lavina Fielding Anderson's creative description: "As apples ripened in

---

1. Lucien Febvre, *Un Destin. Martin Luther* (Paris: Presses Universitaires, 1928). English translation, *Martin Luther: A Destiny* (New York, 1928). It is purely coincidental, but once in an informal conversation at a conference, Quinn suggested that many Mormons resembled late medieval Christians "in a frenzy of religious devotion that was less and less satisfying to them," and James Allen asked him, "Do you see yourself as a modern Luther who will post your own 95 theses about Mormonism?" Quinn, "Chosen Path: A Gay Chicano's Odyssey in Mormon History," 172, unpublished manuscript in my possession.

Utah Valley orchards, the script of the Quinn family's life looked prosperous and rosy: a prestigious academic degree, a secure academic future, a perfectly gender-balanced family of healthy sons and daughters, deep involvement in their Mormon ward, and thriving friendships among Mormonism's scholarly community." Quinn particularly remembered their family and church life that first decade at BYU in idyllic terms, with their life consisting of "daily family prayer with the children at dinner time, regular prayer as a couple every night, earnest individual prayers several times daily, weekly family home evenings, reading the Book of Mormon each Sunday as a family, regular attendance as a family at all LDS meetings, fasting and prayer more than monthly as a couple, [and] frequent temple attendance together," so that, he recalled, "many people had told us we were a 'perfect Mormon couple.'"[2] Similarly, Quinn's BYU career was successful and rewarding: a popular teacher and colleague, he published sufficiently to gain tenure and promotion and became the history department's director of Graduate Studies.

One minor frustration was the fact that BYU was located in Utah Valley. "Jan and I regarded the Provo–Orem area as a cultural wasteland and had no intention of moving there," Quinn remembered (he had, we recall, spent his undergraduate years there). So they remained in the Avenues neighborhood in Salt Lake City and Quinn made the hundred-mile round trip commute three to five times a week. Others, like his mentor Leonard Arrington, made the same decision in the early 1980s when what had been the History Division was transferred to BYU. Quinn made the choice mostly without complaint, with the one exception that he missed the university's evening screenings of international films.[3]

For those prescient enough to know where to look, though, there had always been portents of the turbulence into which his career would descend. For one thing, "whether by earthly design, or one of God's little jokes," the LDS apostle who gave Quinn his

---

2. Lavina Fielding Anderson, "DNA Mormon: D. Michael Quinn," in John Sillito and Susan Staker, eds., *Mormon Mavericks: Essays on Dissenters* (Salt Lake City: Signature Books, 2002), 336; Quinn, "Chosen Path," 208.

3. Quinn, "Chosen Path," 164.

pre-employment interview to determine his worthiness to serve on the BYU faculty was Boyd K. Packer, who would become one of his implacable opponents over the issue of academic freedom and the obligation of the historian to seek the full truth even if it should be inconvenient to the orthodox. What was supposed to be an interview turned out to be about a forty-five-minute lecture in which, according to Quinn's recollection, Packer indicated, among other things, that he had "a hard time with historians because they idolize the truth. The truth is not uplifting; it destroys. I could tell most of the secretaries in the Church Administrative Building that they are ugly and fat. That would be the truth, but it would hurt and destroy them. Historians should tell only that part of the truth that is inspiring and uplifting." Quinn's impression was that Packer "was candid; I was guarded. I spoke of balance, perspective, context. He just shook his head and said, 'You'll learn.' I did."[4]

In addition, although Packer would not have known this, Quinn's research was already venturing into what he called "history's silences." Those silences, for the most part, were mute because they were potentially embarrassing to the orthodox interpretation of Mormon history. For one thing, ever since his undergraduate days, Quinn had been investigating what turned out to be hundreds of plural marriages authorized after 1890, when the marriages were supposedly stopped by official decree. When he published that research in *Dialogue* magazine, it provoked a scandal that led directly to his excommunication. Also, his graduate school research into the Mormon hierarchy produced some controversy when, for example, he documented that Joseph Smith had altered Mormonism's sacred texts to bring them into conformity with his later thinking as the church developed. And only a year into his BYU professorship, he would discover, during a visit to the home of LDS Patriarch Eldred Smith, documentation of Hyrum Smith's practice of the occult arts, which would lead to Quinn's study of *Early Mormonism and the Magic World View*.

Underlying all these potents, though, was the fundamental nature of Quinn's personality, in his dogged insistence on discovering and publishing, in his own way, the full, unsanitized truth of Mormon

---

4. Quinn, "Chosen Path," 162.

history and his naive assumption that readers would agree that a fuller understanding of that truth would not threaten their faith. That prickly stubbornness would inevitably bring him into conflict with any unexamined orthodoxy. Events would demonstrate that Quinn's unwavering faith in the truth of Mormonism, which he maintained all through his excommunication and indeed to the grave, was stronger than that of his persecutors. But in the fall of 1976 that revelation was still long in the future.

For the better part of a decade, then, Quinn's life and career at BYU were ostensibly, at least, happy and productive, with potential problems bottled up or roiling only beneath the surface. But then things began to fall apart: his divorce in 1985, his resignation from the university in 1988, and his excommunication in 1993. In less than a decade, Quinn had become exiled from his marriage, exiled from his academic career, and exiled from the very church that had nurtured him from youth.

First, the divorce. It is not an uncommon story, both within Mormonism and outside it: a gay person, perhaps not yet even fully realizing their sexual orientation and the power it can exert, decides to conform to societal norms and marries a person of the opposite sex, perhaps even having children. Over time, though, the same-sex urges come to the fore and can no longer be ignored, and the resulting incompatibility drives the couple to divorce.

All marriages have occasional conflicts that have to be resolved, and the Quinns' marriage, whatever it might have looked like from the outside, had neither been consistently happy nor unhappy. There had been enough happiness, in fact, that Quinn for a long time could convince himself that his self-deception was working. As a young man, he had dated extensively, but quickly settled on Jan Darley after meeting her—"The first one for whom I felt immediate sexual attraction"—and proposed after the third date. In time the union would produce four children, and there were times of genuine, if a bit clouded, sexual satisfaction. One instance during his army service was particularly memorable: "Berchtesgaden was the most beautiful place I had ever seen. I felt overwhelming and hopeless love for my wife Jan as she and I walked hand-in-hand along the full distance of the lake's shore. Back in the hotel we made love and both shed tears

(I think for different reasons). Nine months later our second child Lisa was born in Munich."[5]

But it could not last, and after several years Quinn was coming to recognize that his hypocrisy was creating insurmountable problems. "It became evident that the struggle I thought I could endure alone had created a marriage of love, devotion, frustration, pain, and increasing despair for us both, as well as growing resentment on her part against me. A heavy price for a girl to pay to fulfill a Mormon boy's sense of duty."[6] Even Jan bought into the deception after he divulged, in 1972, that he was gay. Like a good Mormon foot soldier, she thought that their love and commitment to each other and to their religion could bring them through. "After the initial shock," Quinn remembered, "Jan was determined that we would work out the situation together with our mutual love, devotion, and religious faith."[7]

By 1976, when Quinn began his tenure at BYU and people were observing how idyllic their marriage seemed to be, it was, in fact, increasingly in a shambles and Jan was "on the verge of asking me for a divorce." At that desperate moment, the couple met individually with LDS Church leader Marion D. Hanks, a member of the Presidency of the First Quorum of the Seventy and Quinn's former mission president who had performed their temple wedding. "President Hanks was compassionate and supportive toward me," Quinn recalled. "He said that he knew of no cure for homosexuality and disagreed with LDS leaders who told young men that their homosexual desires would disappear when they married." As wise as that was, Hanks had no advice that would save their marriage, and only advised Quinn that no church leaders (specifically naming Boyd K. Packer) had a right to question him about his sexual orientation and told him, in the interest of protecting his BYU faculty position and leadership roles in the church, to deny his homosexuality, if asked. So those meetings turned out to be futile, and, in fact, things were made worse when Quinn recorded them in his journal and Jan worried

---

5. Quinn, "Chosen Path," 94–95, 118.
6. Quinn, "Chosen Path," 94–95.
7. Quinn, "Chosen Path," 134.

that their children might read there about his homosexuality. Quinn bowed to her wishes and tore out those pages.[8]

Eventually, on Easter Sunday 1985, the Quinns told their children that they were divorcing and that Michael would be moving elsewhere within a month. As the couple had carefully hidden their marital problems from the children, the news was shocking. And it was equally surprising to their friends who had considered them "the perfect Mormon couple." Most curious, perhaps, was the reaction of Quinn's parents, who themselves had divorced when he was five years old, who had both divorced a second time and were struggling with difficult third marriages, and should have been in a good place to understand their son's predicament. "Instead, they expressed disappointment in me, and agreed with Jan's parents that I was selfish. I had always lived to be the shining knight of my family, but I had also feared that they could not accept me without my exemplary Mormon armor. There was no joy in learning I was right."[9]

When the divorce decree came in January 1986, Quinn welcomed it because "I felt it provided [Jan] the only possibility for happiness and fulfillment. I didn't think it much mattered for me." Jan did indeed move on to that happiness and fulfillment, but she found it outside Utah and outside the Mormon Church. By 1987 she and the children were gone from both. She urged Michael to find sexual and emotional satisfaction with a male partner and even assured him that if his family and friends could not accept that, he was always welcome to spend holidays like Thanksgiving with her and their children. That, in fact, turned out to be what happened, and his children after his death fondly remember a father who "always joined us for holidays so we were a complete family, flying to Montana blizzards from New Orleans … , flying to Salt Lake from LA, meeting us in the San Juan Islands, or simply joining us from down the street."[10]

For Quinn, who decided to stay in his existing personal, church, and professional environments, things became more and more rough. Roy Darley, his former father-in-law whose conformity to Mormon

---

8. Quinn, "Chosen Path," 163–64.
9. Quinn, "Chosen Path," 207–208.
10. Quinn, "Chosen Path," 224, 239–39; *Salt Lake Tribune*, Apr. 26, 2021

expectations had alienated his son and intimidated his daughter Jan, was predictably harsh. He told Quinn he was "the most selfish person he had ever known," adding that "I don't hate you, Mike; I pity you." "Pity is better than hatred," Quinn observed, "but I thought I was living the life that would avoid either." A former missionary companion, whom he considered his best friend, wrote to him condemning him for the divorce. Later, after two years of no contact, the former companion wrote to say that there were things he would never be able to understand, but that "he would always be my friend. I thanked him," Quinn said, "but decided not to say I didn't regard grudging toleration as friendship."[11]

Even his colleagues in the BYU history department harassed him. James Allen, the department chair, queried him about Jan's lack of church attendance—a question Quinn could not answer because they were no longer living together. Allen also noted that Quinn had been seen dancing at a gay bar in Salt Lake City, and Quinn could respond that he had been there on a group date, and that the attendees had been about half gay and half straight. Allen added that he disliked receiving such information and advised, "Just be careful, Mike; people are watching you." Quinn later learned that things were even more sinister, and that both BYU security and LDS security had had him under surveillance during his last years at BYU.[12]

Quinn's second exile was the loss of his academic career.

When Apostle Howard W. Hunter succeeded Apostle Joseph Fielding Smith as Church Historian and Recorder in 1970, he almost completely opened the LDS Church Archives. It was a momentous event in Mormon historiography, for suddenly the pent-up energies of historians who had been hobbled by Smith's restrictive policies were free to explore at will over the mostly virgin land of official church records. Equally significant was the creation in 1972 of the History Division under the direction of professional historian Leonard J. Arrington, the purpose of which was to research, write, edit and publish Mormon history under the official auspices of the LDS Church. When Arrington gathered about him a staff of ambitious historians, mostly young and with PhD's from prestigious

11. Quinn, "Chosen Path," 236–37.
12. Quinn, "Chosen Path," 226–30.

institutions (a staff that eventually, though briefly, included Quinn), it inaugurated a period often euphorically, if also simplistically, called the "Arrington Spring," in which the church itself was seen as promoting thoroughly researched, honest, objective history.[13]

That euphoria was not, however, shared by all, particularly conservative members of the church hierarchy like Apostles Boyd K. Packer, Ezra Taft Benson, and Mark E. Petersen. To them, "objective history" meant publishing unflattering facts about heroic figures of the Mormon past that, they claimed, would erode respect for those leaders and role models among the Mormon rank and file. In particular, they had in mind the very first book issued by the History Division, Dean Jessee's edition of *Letters of Brigham Young to His Sons*, in which Young admonished his namesake son to give up his addiction to tobacco.[14] That opposition continued to build, and resulted, in 1982, in the abolition of the History Division and transfer of its staff to the newly created (and ironically named) Joseph Fielding Smith Institute at Brigham Young University.[15] It was Leonard Arrington's own exile.

On the eve of that banishment, Packer issued a blistering assault on what he called "accurate, objective history of the Church" advocated by academically trained scholars. Called "The Mantle is Far, Far Greater Than the Intellect," it was first given as a talk to personnel in the Church Education System, then published in *Brigham Young University Studies*.[16] (Packer had been a career LDS educator prior to joining the church hierarchy.) The body of the talk was "four cautions" which Packer offered to anyone involved in writing or teaching church history:

> There is no such thing as an accurate, objective history of the Church without consideration of the spiritual powers that attend this work.

---

13. The history of that period is told by Arrington himself in *Adventures of a Church Historian* (Urbana: University of Illinois Press, 1998), and Gregory A. Prince, *Leonard Arrington and the Writing of Mormon History* (Salt Lake City: University of Utah Press, 2016).

14. Dean Jessee, ed., *Letters of Brigham Young to His Sons* (Salt Lake City: Deseret Book Co., 1974). Packer's objections are discussed in Arrington, *Adventures*, 119–21.

15. Arrington, *Adventures*, chap. 14; Prince, *Leonard Arrington*, chaps. 22–23.

16. Boyd K. Packer, "The Mantle is Far, Far Greater Than the Intellect," *Brigham Young University Studies* 21 (Summer 1981): 259–78.

There is a temptation for the writer or the teacher of Church history to want to tell everything, whether it is faith promoting or not.

In an effort to be objective, impartial, and scholarly, a writer or a teacher may unwittingly be giving equal time to the adversary.

The final caution concerns the idea that so long as something is already in print, so long as it is available from another source, there is nothing out of order in using it in writing or speaking or teaching.

Packer named no names, but there was little mystery about the identity of his targets: the History Division and its staff and Mormon scholars everywhere who had taken inspiration from the Arrington Spring and its commitment to balanced, objective interpretation in their own teaching and writing.

Quinn took Packer's criticisms personally. Although he as yet had produced no major publication, he had worked briefly in the History Division, had taken full advantage of the open archives to research publications that would appear in the future, and regarded Leonard Arrington as a close mentor and friend, a father figure, even.[17] Even more than that, though, he considered Packer's speech—rightly— as a frontal assault on the fundamental commitment to objectivity that lies at the base of every academic discipline in the humanities and sciences and is drilled into every history graduate student at the beginning of their training. At about the same time as Packer's talk, other conservative Mormons, including members of the hierarchy, joined the melee: Elders Ezra Taft Benson and Gordon B. Hinckley, and BYU political science professor Louis C. Midgley, Quinn felt compelled to respond, and to respond to them all at once.[18]

---

17. In 1981 Quinn held the rank of Associate Professor—not a junior rank, but not at the highest level either. Although he had written no books, he had written several articles, but only one was in a national journal: "The Mormon Church and the Spanish-American War: An End to Selective Pacifism," *Pacific Historical Review* 43 (Aug. 1974): 342–66.

18. Quinn knew that, as a relatively unknown BYU professor, he was taking a huge risk in rebutting a member of the Quorum of the Twelve. It would be hard, though, to name anyone senior to him who would have been willing to enter the lists. Leonard Arrington eschewed polemics, and neither he nor Davis Bitton nor James Allen, his senior colleagues in the History Division, were risk takers where their church status was concerned. It is also possible that Arrington, Bitton, and Allen disagreed with both Quinn's approach and criticisms.

Quinn's opportunity came in October 1981, when the student president of BYU's chapter of Phi Alpha Theta, the national history honor society, invited him to give his reflections on Packer's article to a meeting of the chapter. Whatever his academic status, Quinn's talk, "On Being a Mormon Historian," is nothing short of a masterpiece of exposition and defense of historical method.[19] Perhaps unwittingly, Quinn was applying St. Anselm's principle of "faith seeking understanding" to Mormon history.[20] Faith and reason are not at war, he was saying, even though Packer and others were trying to fire the first shot.

One of Quinn's finest pieces of writing, in my opinion, the penetrating logic and apt examples of "On Being a Mormon Historian" can be fully appreciated only by direct reading. To summarize it briefly, though, Quinn makes three basic points about the kind of "faith-promoting" history that Packer was presumably insisting upon: for one thing, it is dishonest; for another, it is unrealistic; and finally, it is potentially faith-damaging rather than faith-promoting.

On Packer's criticism of historians' "exaggerated loyalty to the theory that everything must be told," for example, Quinn answers: "If I were to write about any subject unrelated to religion and I purposely failed to make reference to pertinent information of which I had knowledge, I would be justifiably criticized for dishonesty." Similarly, he chides Packer, along with some others for insisting upon simple, one-sided, "monistic" explanations of people and events at the expense of more realistic, multi-faceted, "pluralistic" explanations: "They ask that any interpreter simply change the monistic category of Joseph Smith as fraud, or religious genius, or personality disorder, for the equally monistic interpretation that Joseph Smith was a divine prophet." Quinn's dissatisfaction with monism extends

---

19. Quinn's talk was eventually published in an expanded version as "On Being a Mormon Historian (and Its Aftermath)," in George D. Smith, ed., *Faithful History: Essays on Writing Mormon History* (Salt Lake City: Signature Books, 1992), 69–111. Footnotes 8, 9 and 11, pp. 98–99, give complete citations to the attacks Quinn was addressing. The reader is also directed to Lavina Fielding Anderson's "DNA Mormon: D. Michael Quinn," which covers the same ground I am about to enter here, with additional details and a slightly different point of view.

20. See, for example, Frederick Copleston, S.J., *A History of Philosophy, Volume 2: Medieval Philosophy, Volume 1: Augustine to Bonaventure* (Garden City, NY: Doubleday Image Books, 1962), chap. 15, esp. p. 177.

to events as well as people: "Personally, I am not willing to simply say that 'the hand of the Lord' is sufficient explanation for all events and developments in the Mormon past." Even sacred writings, he goes on, do not happen monistically: "Sacred history presents God's leaders as understandable human beings with whom the reader can identify because of their weaknesses at the same time the reader reveres the prophetic mantle. ... In fact, the scriptures do exactly what Elder Packer condemns."[21]

Finally, Quinn points out that Packer's "faith-promoting" history actually risks becoming faith-damaging: "So-called 'faith-promoting' church history which conceals controversies and difficulties of the Mormon past may actually undermine the faith of Latter-day Saints who eventually learn about the problems from other sources."[22] In support, he uses the example of the church's cover-up of post-1890 Manifesto polygamy which Quinn had first discovered as a BYU undergraduate. "Historians," he concludes, "do not create problem areas of the Mormon past, but most of us cannot agree to conceal them, either. We are trying to respond to those problem areas of Mormon experience. Attacking the messenger does not alter the reality of the message."[23]

It was an eloquent defense of historical objectivity and honesty, and any academically trained scholar would agree that Quinn carried the day in the debate. What Quinn apparently did not reckon with was Packer's long memory. Quinn's former mission president Marion D. Hanks warned him that "Boyd K. Packer was easily offended, never forgot anyone who challenged him, and would remain vindictive years afterward. ... 'It may take him years,' Hanks added, 'but he will get his vengeance on you.'"[24] Gordon B. Hinckley, an apostle and member of the First Presidency, privately warned Quinn: "I am gravely concerned that you have publicly criticized living members of the Quorum of the Twelve." Quinn "explained that I didn't intend this as a personal criticism of these apostles. I felt that I had the right as a historian to evaluate their public views

---

21. Quinn, "On Being," 76–77, 79–80.
22. Quinn, "On Being," 87.
23. Quin, "On Being," 87–88.
24. Quinn, "Chosen Path," 191.

on how Church history should be written." Hinckley persisted: "Of course you have that right, Brother Quinn, ... but when you do it publicly, that can sow seeds of dissension among Church members." Quinn, still unable to foresee the tempest that Hinckley clearly had in view, replied that "that wasn't my intent."[25] Quinn's eyes would be opened soon enough.

Any hope of comity between the two—Packer and Quinn—was dashed early in 1982 when Kenneth L. Woodward, a reporter for *Newsweek*, picked up the story of Quinn's rebuttal to Packer and made it a national *cause célèbre*. One doubts that the reportedly thin-skinned Packer could have gotten over what he regarded as Quinn's affront even if the incident had been contained to the local level. But Woodward cast the confrontation almost as Quinn's Galileo going up against Packer's Urban VIII—science versus obscurantism—a drama in which no one would want to play the villain's role. "By last week," Woodward wrote, "it appeared that Quinn's counterattack had put [Elder Ezra Taft] Benson and Packer on the defensive. ... If faith in Mormonism means faith in the church's history, then they [the historians] would seem to have the edge over their adversaries."[26]

Although, as Woodward points out, "a few other LDS historians have complained privately to the apostles," few of those who sided with Quinn were brave enough to go public with their views. One who did was Clifton Jolley, a boyhood friend of Quinn and a college roommate. Jolley remembered Quinn as completely uncontroversial and an icon of "stability and sensibility" and thus an unlikely lightning rod for Packer's wrath. "The whole thing is quite ironic," Quinn told Jolley. "I sort of backed into history as a profession, not because I particularly cared for history, but because I saw it as a means of understanding and defending my church." Woodward, therefore, "didn't do Michael any favors" by inflating to national importance "what even Michael calls an 'in-house issue'" Consequently, Jolley concluded, in what turned out to be an egregiously inaccurate prediction, "I suspect that in a few weeks the whole thing will be

---

25. Quinn, "Background and Fallout of My 1985 Article 'LDS Church Authority and New Plural Marriages, 1890–1904,'" *Sunstone* 179 (Fall 2015): 16.

26. Kenneth L. Woodward, "Apostles Vs. Historians," *Newsweek*, Feb. 15, 1982, 77.

forgotten, as is most of what *Newsweek* gives peripheral attention."[27] In fact, "in a few weeks," instead of going away, the confrontation flared up again.

Quinn's first book, *J. Reuben Clark: The Church Years,* was commissioned by the Clark family and the LDS Church, and was to be an officially sanctioned companion to Frank W. Fox's lengthy study of Clark's career in law and diplomacy. Though deemed acceptable by the family, the manuscript provoked opposition within the church hierarchy. Leading the attack was Francis M. Gibbons, secretary to the First Presidency and himself author of uncritical, near-hagiographic studies of prominent Mormon leaders. Gibbons reported that the manuscript had deeply upset Clark's old friend, Apostle Marion G. Romney, and "was finally cleared for publication only after numerous items had been changed or deleted." Gibbons added that "the manuscript as originally submitted probably would have had the approval of the warts-and-all school of biography"— indicating a level of objectivity of which Gibbons did not approve. Although Quinn had heard a diametrically opposite report that Romney had considered that "it captured the essence of President Clark's personality and church service," he agreed to "numerous deletions and revisions" to the first draft.[28]

Evidently, that was not good enough for Packer. Still feeling the sting of Quinn's "On Being a Mormon Historian," Packer asserted that Quinn's book "dirties the public memory of J. Reuben Clark," and added: "As sure as I am sitting in this chair, Mike Quinn's book on President Clark will never see the light of day." "It was no idle threat," Quinn realized, "since this was an official biography scheduled to be published by BYU Press." Although Quinn had told no one what he had heard of Packer's opposition, Packer had apparently broadcast his opinion around church headquarters. Consequently, the First Presidency appointed two of Packer's ecclesiastical superiors, apostles Howard W. Hunter and Thomas S. Monson, to give the manuscript a final review. Their recommendation was that Quinn change "sensational quotes into paraphrases" and limit "the examples

---

27. Clifton Jolley, "*Newsweek* Put Him in the Middle," *Deseret News,* Feb. 12, 1982.

28. Quinn, *Elder Statesman: A Biography of J. Reuben Clark* (Salt Lake City: Signature Books, 2002), vii–ix.

of conflict and controversy in the First Presidency's office." "However," Quinn added, they "let the basic conflicts and controversies remain in the manuscript. I've always admired them for that."[29]

When the book actually came out, Quinn was leading a BYU study abroad program in Austria, and was thus dependent on friends like Leonard Arrington to track its reception and report to him. Its appearance coincided with the church's spring general conference, and in a promotional effort, the BYU bookstore was selling it at a steep discount, where Arrington got his own copy. When Arrington chided architectural historian Paul Anderson for paying full price at Deseret Book, Anderson replied, "I don't care what it cost[.] I wanted to get a copy before they removed it from the shelves!" "So you see," Arrington added to Quinn, "there is some fear and trembling about this sort of thing. As I say[,] the comments I have heard came primarily from historians at BYU and elsewhere, and all of them are very positive."[30]

All of this, though, had taken place mostly behind the scenes, and was little more than a warm-up for the academic and ecclesiastical conflagration that Quinn would ignite with his 1985 study of post-Manifesto polygamy.[31] From an early age, Quinn had been aware of polygamy as an element in Mormon history, had known people descended from polygamous marriages, and, in contrast with most modern mainstream Mormons, actually believed in the divinity of the principle. While in the army, he had met an Egyptian Mormon who practiced polygamy, which was legal in his country. Later, back in Utah, Quinn became familiar with members of several modern polygamous sects that had grown out of Mormonism. And, as we have seen, he had begun his first studies of the history of polygamy while an undergraduate at BYU, provoked by the outrage of a fellow student at a religion professor who had called his post-Manifesto polygamist ancestors "apostates."[32]

---

29. Quinn, "Chosen Path," 198–99.

30. Arrington to Quinn, Mar. 31, 1983, Leonard James Arrington Papers, Special Collections, Merrill-Cazier Library, Utah State University, Logan.

31. Quinn, "LDS Authority and New Plural Marriages, 1890–1904," *Dialogue: A Journal of Mormon Thought* 18 (Spring 1985): 9–105.

32. Quinn, "Background and Fallout," 6–7. Signature Books in Salt Lake City holds a pre-publication draft of this article that Quinn had given the previous spring as a talk to a Mormon Fundamentalist group in Centennial Park, Arizona.

Over the years, Quinn had continued his study of post-Manifesto polygamy, but with little intention to publish it. In January 1979, he began to put it all together. Responding hurriedly and informally, without access to his notes, to a request from G. Homer Durham, managing director of the Historical Department of the Church, for a summary of post-Manifesto polygamy that Durham could share with the First Presidency, Quinn produced a twelve-page, single-spaced document. As he submitted it, he informed Durham that he was violating a pact he had made with himself years previously that he would never speak or publish on the subject of polygamy until he could be sure that he had seen all the relevant sources and was thus certain that he was telling the entire story and correctly interpreting it. He had brought himself to this violation, he explained, only because the request had come from the First Presidency.[33]

Events, though, were pulling him in the direction of preparing just such a study. A 1980 article by Victor W. Jorgensen and B. Carmon Hardy in the *Utah Historical Quarterly*,[34] which Quinn regarded as incomplete in research, as distorting in interpretation, and possibly as causing some faithful Mormons to blame the church for having lied to them (as he had warned in "On Being a Mormon Historian"), spurred him to take up his polygamy research in earnest in order to complete and correct the record—and to defend the church he loved. He was unwittingly putting himself on a trajectory that would lead instead to excommunication from that very church.

First, though, he would need unrestricted access to documents the church had tightly guarded from historians. Durham had been so impressed with Quinn's twelve-page summary that he had quietly given Quinn access to such restricted documents as he could, but Quinn knew there were others in the First Presidency's office vault—a repository separate from the holdings of LDS Archives—that he would need in order to do the job properly. Accordingly, he approached the First Presidency directly in a two-page letter of May 20, 1980, alerting them of the appearance of the Jorgensen-Hardy article and pressing upon them the urgent need for a thoroughly

---

33. Quinn," Background and Fallout," 13.

34. Victor W. Jorgensen and B. Carmon Hardy, "The Taylor-Cowley Affair and the Watershed of Mormon History," *Utah Historical Quarterly* 48 (Winter 1980): 4–36.

documented study from within the church that would make a clean breast of the controversial subject. To justify the project, Quinn quoted J. Reuben Clark, whose biography he was writing, to the effect that "one of the reasons why the so-called 'Fundamentalists' have made such inroads among our young people was because we had failed to teach them the truth." "Up to the present," Quinn added, "there has not been available to the members of the Church a documented, full history that enables them to distinguish between unauthorized and authorized plural marriage." Lacking that history, "tens of thousands of Latter-day Saints will be increasingly vulnerable targets for polygamist cultists."

Quinn went on to state that his research has discovered more than 200 authorized plural marriages between 1890 and 1904, with some 70,000 descendants today. "I am sure," he commented, "that most of these faithful Latter-day Saints (some of them your own children and grandchildren) cannot explain why it is wrong for them to enter polygamy today when it was right for their ancestors to marry in polygamy after the Manifesto." The history Quinn proposed would show that both authorized and unauthorized plural marriages occurred throughout Mormon history and that church leaders all the way back to Joseph Smith approved the former and condemned the latter.[35]

Realizing that on the larger scale of things, a brash, presumptuous associate professor at BYU might appear as a nobody to the First Presidency, Quinn cited, without first seeking their permission, G. Homer Durham and Leonard Arrington as witnesses to the quality of his work as a historian and his status as a faithful Latter-day Saint. Writing a bit sheepishly to Arrington as he sent him a copy of the First Presidency letter, Quinn said, "I know that if I had consulted you for advice about this letter, that you would have advised me against sending it to the Presidency. I have done enough years of research in First Presidency correspondence and other documents," he added, "to know that they take an extremely dim view of unsolicited advice, especially when it comes from someone of no Church importance or significant administrative experience." "I have no way

---

35. Quinn to First Presidency, May 20, 1980, copy in Arrington Papers.

of predicting the exact results of my letter. ... Perhaps they will ignore it completely. ... At any event, I have done what is in my power (which isn't very much) to do about a matter that I feel is a cancer at the center of the Church. The rest I must leave to the Lord and to his servants."[36]

Even before appealing to the First Presidency, Quinn figured they would likely deny him access to the sources he was seeking, and was coming to the decision that he was going to publish his polygamy research anyway, based on the extensive evidence he already had. On July 19, 1979, he confided in his journal, "Since it appears that the First Presidency will never allow the crucial documents to be made available for an honest exploration of this matter, I may present what I presently understand for whatever benefit it may have to the Church membership in understanding." Already, too, Quinn had come to the realization that martyrdom, both academic and ecclesiastical, probably awaited him: publishing the polygamy article "will probably end my career at BYU. ... [but] Such an article on the significance of the 1890 Manifesto would not be a bad Last Hurrah for me as a Mormon historian. After that, I can foresee nothing of significance or fulfillment." Even more, "I am now sure that if I write the kind of article that I feel must be written and publish it in *Dialogue* as I plan to do ... , that there is no power on earth that will spare me from excommunication if Mark E. Petersen is alive. ... I am approaching the point," he concluded, "where I would prefer to have my collision with the authorities over this matter, and then take whatever consequences may follow."[37] The depth of his resolution came out in a private conversation with historian Gregory Prince, who asked him how he could publish such audacious things "and still get away with it." Quinn's response was immediate: "Because I don't give a damn."[38]

Predictably, once Quinn's 97-page essay appeared in the April 1985 issue of *Dialogue*, reactions among the church hierarchy were swift. Packer, in several public meetings, denounced Quinn

---

36. Quinn to Arrington, May 20, 1980, Arrington Papers.
37. Quinn, Journal, July 19 and Oct. 31, 1979, in Quinn, "Background and Fallout," 15, 16.
38. Quinn, "Background and Fallout," 16.

anonymously as "a BYU historian who is writing about polygamy to embarrass the Church." In a meeting of the Quorum of the Twelve, he attacked Quinn by name and accused him of apostasy: "What Mike Quinn wrote about plural marriage may be true, but no faithful Latter-day Saint would publish what he did."[39]

Assaults even came from an unexpected quarter: Apostle Dallin H. Oaks "formerly my congenial friend while he was president of BYU," Quinn characterized him. Oaks's criticism actually had little substance; he just felt personally betrayed because Quinn had not divulged to him, when he was BYU president, the restricted sources he was using and advised him that he was going to publish. Quinn's response was that he had gained access to those sources by authorization from G. Homer Durham and had informed Durham and members of the First Presidency that he was going to write the article. "I had volunteered those details to the general authorities who had a right to know," Quinn informed Oaks, "—a *need* to know about my knowledge about post-Manifesto polygamy."[40]

From that point, the dual attack launched by Packer on the premise that Quinn was both a bad historian and a bad Mormon proceeded in tandem. In May 1985 three apostles, whom Quinn correctly guessed were Elders Packer, Neal A. Maxwell, and Dallin H. Oaks, ordered Quinn's regional president, James M. Paramore, to have Quinn's stake president, Hugh S. West, confiscate Quinn's temple recommend. The charge was that Quinn had "spoken evil of the Lord's anointed" by asserting that the First Presidency had approved post-Manifesto polygamy. West was also instructed to "take further action" if pulling the temple recommend failed to silence Quinn. Finally, West was ordered to lie to Quinn that the order had originated with West, not the higher authorities. Throughout a two-hour meeting, West—a man of integrity—refused to lie and argued strongly against the decision itself. He himself had read Quinn's article and saw nothing in it that would justify disciplinary action. In the end, though, he bowed to authority and asked Quinn for his recommend.[41]

---

39. Quinn, "Background and Fallout," 17.
40. Quinn, "Background and Fallout," 17–18.
41. Quinn, "Background and Fallout," 18.

Losing his recommend "*really* hurt," Quinn recalled, "because I had been a regularly scheduled ordinance-worker in the temple one day each week." There was, of course, much more at stake than Quinn's temple participation. "The stake president told me," Quinn remembered, "that he regarded his instructions from Church headquarters as a back-door effort to have me fired at BYU." West decided, though, to follow the letter of the law only. In order to protect Quinn's employment, he took the recommend and put it into his desk drawer so that if anyone at the university asked him if he had a temple recommend, he could say that he did, but be careful at the same time not to divulge that it was in his stake president's desk. Further, West promised to renew the recommend annually. And he allowed Quinn to continue as a counselor in the stake's Sunday school presidency and to continue as a gospel doctrine teacher in his ward.[42]

Quinn, of course, was crushed. True, he had retained his academic position, but at the cost of having to accept an attenuated participation in Mormonism. "You'll just have to live without the temple," West told him by way of consolation. "More than once in 1985," Quinn remembered, "I left his office knowing that the temple was not the only part of Mormonism I must learn to live without. … That was the end of my Mormon dreams." "From 1985 onward it was obvious to me that my life in the LDS Church would be over. …The life I had lived-for was over and just hadn't fallen over yet. I continued teaching, researching, writing, living, but wondered why I bothered. I was losing everything and everyone I valued after doing everything I had thought God wanted me to do."[43]

By this time, Quinn's experience at BYU had become one of extremes. Almost simultaneously, as Joseph Fielding McConkie, a professor of religion, was reportedly denouncing Quinn at local ward firesides both in California and Utah as "the Anti-Christ of BYU," graduating seniors in the history department voted him "Outstanding Teacher." Even more ominously for Quinn's future research, the Historical Department of the Church began, at Packer's order, to require researchers to sign a form agreeing to church censorship before publication of anything they had written based on church

---

42. Quinn, "Background and Fallout," 18–19.
43. Quinn," Background and Fallout," 18–19; Quinn, "Chosen Path," 220, 224.

archives. The censorship was retroactive on any research conducted even before signing the form. It was "an effort," Quinn recognized, "to retroactively close the door on the previous sixteen years of openness in the LDS Church Archives," and, of course, he refused to sign. His refusal opened the door for Packer to claim, hypocritically, that "we did not exclude Mike Quinn from the archives. He excluded himself."[44] Quinn, of course, could continue to publish based on the years of research he had already completed, but further access to the archives would be denied. The noose was tightening.

Personal harassment followed, including reported incidents of spying on him by both the university and the church. His department chair at BYU grilled him on his ex-wife's and his children's church activity. Such prying into his family's affairs drove him to distraction: "I felt like yelling at the top of my lungs that if I didn't have a right to privacy because I was a controversial Mormon historian, my ex-wife certainly had that right. She should not be scrutinized, gossiped about, or reported upon simply because of her connection with me. I had always loved the closeness of Mormon culture, but for the first time I realized that the LDS Church can be suffocatingly intrusive in people's lives."[45]

Before long, the spying struck even closer, and soon his department chair was advising him: "Just be careful, Mike, people are watching you." Quinn learned that both BYU Security and LDS Church Security had placed him under surveillance both in Provo and Salt Lake City. Quinn took the news with remarkable equanimity. Although he realized that the surveillance was being conducted with the goal of either getting him fired from BYU or forcing him to resign, "I didn't feel any concern about the surveillance," he said, "because I was celibate and adhering to LDS standards, even if I was unconventional."[46]

Pressures on his research and writing mounted. After giving a paper on the church's business activities (research which would be expanded in 2017 into *The Mormon Hierarchy: Wealth and Corporate Power*), Quinn received a distraught telephone call at home from his dean, informing him that he, the dean, "had been instructed 'by

44. Quinn, "Chosen Path," 225–26.
45. Quinn, "Chosen Path," 227.
46. Quinn, "Chosen Path," 228–29.

higher authority'" to order Quinn not to publish the paper. When Quinn protested that the paper had not been based on any archival records, but rather on publicly accessible documents, the dean responded that he realized that, but that the order not to publish would have to stand.[47]

It was the beginning of the end of Quinn's academic career. In the fall of 1986, the new dean of his college regretfully informed Quinn that BYU's Executive Committee of Trustees (which included Packer) had decided that he would receive no more sabbaticals or financial support beyond his salary as a faculty member. "I have always hoped," the new dean told Quinn, "that one day BYU will become a *real* university, but makes me feel that day will never arrive." Accordingly, Quinn was removed from a BYU program celebrating 150 years of Mormonism in Britain. Even more than that, it became evident that he would not be receiving support from the university even on non-Mormon research projects. On December 11, 1986, Quinn received an unsolicited invitation to give a paper at the University of Paris in a symposium on the history of magic. The paper made no mention of Mormonism, and Quinn had been given to understand that the university would cover his expenses, but BYU reneged, and Quinn had to pay his own way to a conference where he would be representing the very university that denied him support.[48]

"My career at BYU was finished if I continued my work as a Mormon historian, and yet that's why I went there," Quinn concluded. "The most I could hope for was an uneasy truce if I agreed not to publish any more history that might offend the Brethren. ... Abandoning Mormon history was safe in the current climate of repression, but was unacceptable to me, especially as an option of duress. 'Publish or perish' is the experience of scholars at most universities, but for this Mormon historian it was 'publish and perish' at BYU."[49]

Further difficulties came from an unexpected quarter as pre-publication reviews began in 1987 for his book on early Mormonism and

---

47. Quinn, "Chosen Path," 204–205.

48. Quinn, "Chosen Path," 231. Quinn to Viola Sachs, Dec. 22, 1986, copy in Arrington Papers. In an undated fragment in the Arrington Papers, Quinn apparently solicited support from Arrington to meet part of the $1,935 estimated total expense of the trip. It is unclear if Quinn received that support.

49. Quinn, "Chosen Path," 231–32.

magic. Reviewing the manuscript for Signature Books, Quinn's former mentor Davis Bitton "made some helpful criticisms, but most of his review was a plea to me and the publisher to abandon this project. He said that my study was an assault on the faith of average Latter-day Saints. If I insist on publishing this book, Davis instructed me not to mention in the acknowledgments that he had read the manuscript." Bitton's turnabout sent Quinn into a period of depression that lasted several weeks. Things were not helped by the fact that he had gotten similar criticisms from two other readers he had also considered to be supporters: "My second book," Quinn lamented, "and now it's defenders of the New Mormon History who want me not to publish! I guess I am a radical, even though I've never felt like one."[50]

When the magic book did appear, it triggered rumors within the history department and the university that Quinn was going to be fired and excommunicated as well. Although his dean assured him that they were only rumors, it was clear that Quinn was the odd man out and that tensions between him, his ecclesiastical superiors, and the university were reaching an untenable point. One of his students asked him if he should change his history major to something else. "Mike, the Church is my life, and I don't want to wind up like you," he said. "His honesty hurt," Quinn said, "but I couldn't blame him. I felt I had no alternative but to leave BYU as soon as possible. If I'd ever belonged there, that time was past."[51]

Worrying that he had become a poison property and that friends and colleagues were being cast under suspicion through association with him, Quinn began divesting himself of professional and church positions outside of his professorship. Accordingly, he resigned from the governing council of the Mormon History Association and the board of editors of *Dialogue* magazine. Similarly, he resigned as gospel doctrine teacher in his LDS ward, despite protests from fellow ward members who considered him the best teacher in the ward and pleaded with him to stay.[52]

In preparation for his resignation from BYU, Quinn began applying for other positions so that when he left, he would have

---

50. Quinn, "Chosen Path," 232–33.
51. Quinn, "Chosen Path," 234–35.
52. Quinn, "Chosen Path," 239–40.

"something to leave to." Leonard Arrington wrote letters of recommendation for a faculty position at Princeton University; "I can
understand why he would be interested in moving to another university," Arrington admitted. The one that panned out, though, was
his application for a year-long fellowship at the Huntington Library
to work on the expansion of his master's and doctoral theses which
would become the three volumes of *The Mormon Hierarchy*.[53]

With the Huntington fellowship in place, Quinn submitted
his resignation in January 1988 to become effective at the end of
the term in April. "The situation seems to be," he explained in his
resignation letter, "that academic freedom merely survives at BYU
without fundamental support by the institution, exists against tre-
mendous pressure, and is nurtured only through the dedication of
individual administrators and faculty members. It was my formal
acknowledgment of failure—personal and institutional."[54] It was a
damning indictment of the university, but by the following July, it
became apparent that Quinn was actually pulling his punches. At
that time he told a newspaper reporter that "BYU officials have said
that Harvard should aspire to be the BYU of the East. That's like
saying the Mayo Clinic should aspire to be Auschwitz. ... BYU is an
Auschwitz of the mind."[55] It was, of course, hyperbole of the most
extreme kind, for BYU has produced, in all fields including history,
first-rate scholars and has continued to attract the highest quality
students, but it is a telling indicator of Quinn's state of mind at the
time. A more temperate and extensive rejoinder appeared in *Student
Review*, BYU's off-campus student newspaper, under the title "The
Marketplace of Ideas, the House of Faith, and the Prison of Conformity," in which Quinn elaborated his experiences of suppression
of academic freedom and pressure for conformity.[56]

As expected, reactions to his resignation differed. On the one hand,

---

53. Minutes of the Joseph Fielding Smith Institute, Feb. 17, 1988, 1; Leonard Arrington to John M. Murrin, Nov. 3, 1987; Arrington to Martin Ridge, Feb. 3, 1988; all
in Arrington Papers.

54. Quinn, "Chosen Path," 240–41.

55. Quinn, "Chosen Path," 257.

56. Quinn, "The Marketplace of Ideas, the House of Faith, and the Prison of Conformity," *Student Review*, Apr. 6, 1988, 11, 13. The article also appeared, under a slightly
different title, in *Sunstone* 12 (Mar. 1988), 6–7.

there were "expressions of grim satisfaction" within some departments and university administration. Even among his own departmental colleagues, who were "stunned" and objected that he should not have resigned, there was an undercurrent of relief that the department would now be spared the unwelcome scrutiny that their unruly colleague had drawn upon them. The Joseph Fielding Smith Institute (Leonard Arrington's History Division which had been "banished" to BYU in 1982) held a special get-together in Quinn's honor. In addition to the expected well-wishing, there was a dark note: "Referring to Mike Quinn's down-beat assessment of the prospects for Mormon history, Ron Walker asked rhetorically, 'Can we have professional history written in the Church today?'" Leonard Arrington responded, lengthily and with his proverbial rosy outlook, in the affirmative, with examples of ways in which the possibilities for professional history had actually gotten better over the years.[57] But the circumstances leading to the meeting and Quinn's presence there must have cast something of a shadow over Arrington's sometimes facile optimism.

Quinn's parting from BYU was as frustrating as his faculty experience had been. The history department gave him a luncheon and a gift; his college dean asked him to stop by before he left, but was out of town when Quinn called. "The last item on BYU's official checkout form was to be signed by Don Abel, the associate academic vice-president, whose signature was supposed to verify that I had received a 'Termination Interview,'" Quinn wrote to Arrington. "As I stood in the doorway to his office, his secretary handed the form to him, he looked at it, glanced up at me, signed it without a word, and went back to the other paperwork on his desk, as his secretary handed the form back to me. That was the best BYU's administration could cough up after my eleven years on the faculty. There's no love lost on either side."[58]

---

57. Minutes of the Joseph Fielding Smith Institute, 2.

58. Quinn to Arrington, June 21, 1988, Arrington Papers. Arrington to Quinn, June 25, 1988, Arrington Papers, reported: "Your cold treatment upon leaving BYU, I think, is typical. BYU administrators are strong on recruiting faculty but 'cold' to those who leave." Arrington goes on to relate his similar treatment when he left the school. Quinn's and Arrington's treatment may not be unique. However, Arrington does add that he was treated warmly and courteously when he left Utah State University to be Church Historian.

Quinn already knew that getting rid of him at BYU would not satisfy his enemies. If he had not already enraged them enough with the polygamy article, the appearance in 1987 of his Mormonism and magic book certainly did the job, and he knew that they probably would not stop short of excommunication. A rumor circulated in the history department that excommunication proceedings over the magic book had been instituted turned out to be false, "but the rumor was founded in a larger reality," Quinn realized. "Only a supportive and courageous stake presidency had saved me from disfellowship-ping or excommunication in 1987 for the magic book. If I moved from that stake I expected to be an easy target for the bastards at Church headquarters, but I knew that it was necessary to leave BYU and to move from my protective stake. One way or another, it was only a matter of time before my Church experience was over."[59]

The conclusion of Quinn's Huntington Library fellowship in 1989 inaugurated a period of several years of seek-and-evade as Quinn sought to keep his whereabouts unknown to the church authorities who intended to haul him before a church court on charges of speaking evil of the Lord's anointed. That period reflects poorly both on the church authorities who were obviously engaged in a vendetta against a loyal member who had already lost so much and on Quinn himself who could only hope to postpone the inevitable. While living in the French Quarter of New Orleans, Quinn received his mail at a post office box and, of course, never attended church services where he could be identified and excommunicated by local authorities. An associate of the church's Membership Department reportedly attempted to locate him through his mother, represent-ing themselves as a business to which Quinn owed a debt. Then they attempted to cajole Quinn's attorney, who refused to disclose his address under attorney-client confidentiality. Finally, they at-tempted to entrap Quinn through a bogus offer of a gold American Express card which required that he provide his address. Through all of this, no doubt, Quinn's experience in army intelligence helped him play the spy game, but he remembered a Mormon CIA officer

---

59. Quinn to Arrington, July 20, 1988, Arrington Papers. The account of Quinn's excommunication which follows is based in large part on Anderson, "DNA Mormon," which contains a much fuller narrative.

in Germany telling him that "the LDS Church is better at tracking down Mormons who don't want to be found than the Company is in tracking down spies." (The CIA officer himself was on the lam from church authorities and was eventually found.)[60]

When Quinn moved back to Salt Lake City in 1992, he knew he was increasing his vulnerability to being found. Bowing at last to the inevitable, he resolved to hide no longer. But he also resolved not to cooperate; in such a situation as he found himself in, where he had no power, he could at least maintain his dignity by saying no. He took an apartment on Capitol Hill and waited for the church to catch up with him.

This time the Inspector Javert to his Jean Valjean was no longer his regional president, but his new stake president, Paul Hanks, and he no longer had a Hugh S. West to protect him. Hanks, Quinn learned, was employed by the Church Education System. As Lavina Fielding Anderson has pointed out, "This was the mini-empire that Elder Packer had presided over during his own lengthy career as a church employee and the forum he used to launch his attack on the New Mormon History."[61] Despite his protestations to the contrary, Hanks was no friend.

Although Quinn, by this time, had a reputation as a troublemaker, the catalyst for his conflict with Hanks was an article, "Mormon Women Have Had the Priesthood Since 1843," which Quinn had contributed to an anthology of articles on Mormon feminism edited by Maxine Hanks, a distant relative of Paul Hanks.[62] (As things turned out, Maxine would also pay the price of excommunication for her role in that anthology.) As soon as he learned of the article, on February 7, 1993, Hanks dropped by Quinn's apartment unannounced, to find Quinn in bed with influenza and unwilling to let him in or talk with him. Later that day, he wrote Quinn a letter

---

60. Quinn, "Chosen Path," 254.

61. Anderson, "DNA Mormon," 350. See also David Haglund, "The Complicated Life of a Mormon Intellectual," Slate.com, posted Nov. 1, 2012, 6, transcript in possession of Signature Books. Paul Hanks was a nephew of Marion D. Hanks, Quinn's LDS mission president who had presided at Quinn's wedding and had become "a father figure of sorts."

62. Quinn, "Mormon Women Have Had the Priesthood Since 1843," in Maxine Hanks, ed., *Women and Authority: Re-emerging Mormon Feminism* (Salt Lake City: Signature Books, 1992).

asking to visit with him not only about the anthology article but also about some of Quinn's recent statements regarding enforced conformity within the church. Although he attempted to assure Quinn that he was "anxious to help, and save, not hinder," Quinn knew better, especially since Hanks went on to cite the church's *General Handbook of Instructions'* definition of apostasy.[63]

An ensuing correspondence over the next few months did nothing to resolve the matter or even reduce the temperature as Hanks's tone became increasingly threatening. For his part, Quinn defended the honesty of his work as a historian and called out Hanks's uncharitable treatment of a faithful Mormon who had served his church well: "I sincerely hope you never are in the situation of being hunted down by those you regard as prophets, seers, and revelators but who have defined you as expendable. No one is expendable to the Lord."[64] Events were nearing a climax.

On June 6, 1993, Quinn received notice of a disciplinary council, which had decided to disfellowship him, placing him on probation, denying him the sacraments and exercise of his priesthood ministry, and even denying him the right to give his testimony in church. Reluctantly, he brought himself to report this to his sixth-generation Mormon mother. Her response was brutally accurate: "They're chopping you off by inches, aren't they?"[65]

The executioner's axe eventually fell in September. By that time, it was clear that Quinn was going to be part of a larger group to be purged from the church and eventually known as the September Six: Lynne Kanavel Whitesides, Paul Toscano, Maxine Hanks, Avraham Gileadi, and Lavina Fielding Anderson.[66]

Quinn was in California when his disciplinary council met on September 26. On September 30, he phoned Hanks to find out what the decision was. It was, as everyone had anticipated, excommunication. No surprise. The surprise was that Quinn learned the decision had taken six hours. He had faced the simple and straightforward

---

63. Paul Hanks to Quinn, Feb. 7, 1993, in Anderson, "DNA Mormon," 348.
64. Quinn to Paul Hanks, May 25, 1993, in Anderson, "DNA Mormon," 351.
65. Anderson, "DNA Mormon," 353.
66. Anderson, "DNA Mormon," 353–54.

charge of refusing to meet with Hanks or attend the hearing. Why would such a thing take six hours?

The answer came some time later. Quinn had forbade any of his friends from either attending the hearing or mounting any kind of defense. But one of them, Barnard "Barney" Silver, had decided to appear, reading at some length from Quinn's articles and playing recordings of his talks while vigorously rebutting the charge of apostasy. Eventually, as he felt the proceeding slipping out of his control, Hanks in exasperation stated that "Elder Packer had been telephoning him every week to stress the importance of taking action against this renegade Mormon historian and that their responsibility was to 'Sustain the Brethren.'" Silver was excused and the council proceeded at last to its foreordained conclusion.[67]

Michael Quinn's life after his excommunication was an incongruous mixture of productivity and drift. Like that other excommunicated university professor, Martin Luther, who translated the German Bible and kept producing theological writings that further developed his Protestant version of Christianity even as he himself receded from public view, Quinn's exile was the most productive period of his career.[68] In addition to the massive three-volume study of the Mormon hierarchy that grew out of his master's thesis and doctoral dissertation, Quinn issued second editions of his J. Reuben Clark biography and his Mormonism and magic book, the latter so extensively revised and expanded as to constitute a new book. And he topped off his career with his same-sex study that he conceived as the first volume of a longer analysis which he never lived to complete. In view of that record, one could suggest that Quinn's writing career may have actually *begun* with his departure from BYU.

Quinn's controversial life and career burst into public attention once more, briefly, in 2004 when he made several attempts to breach

---

67. Anderson, "DNA Mormon," 354. Barney is the son of inventor Harold Silver and his wife, the writer Madelyn Silver, both of whom had been subjects of commissioned biographies by Leonard Arrington. That he would come to such a vigorous defense of Quinn, Arrington's protégé, is thus explicable, but still remarkable. Gary Topping, *Leonard J. Arrington: A Historian's Life* (Norman, OK: Arthur H. Clark, 2008), 167–69.

68. Anderson, "DNA Mormon," 355–59, summarized that productivity. Slyly commenting on the no doubt unexpected results of Quinn's excommunication, Anderson's late husband, Paul, observed, "Well they certainly silenced *him*"!

the raised drawbridges and deep moats of academia. Although he probably did not realize it at the time, Quinn's resignation from BYU burned not only that bridge but also all the other bridges back into academia. No other institution with a heavily Mormon endowment would dare touch him, including even state institutions with a large Mormon constituency like Utah State University and Arizona State University. The rejection of his bid for a faculty position at the University of Utah in 2004, though, produced not only a large rift in the history department but a public scandal as well when a strong Quinn backer on the faculty went public with allegations of faculty fears of alienating the LDS Church.[69] To make matters as bad as possible, even where the academic drawbridges were still down, Quinn refused to cross them: he was offered faculty positions at no fewer than two community colleges—Salt Lake Community College and College of the Sequoias in Visalia, California—but turned them down because the salaries they could offer were such a small percentage of what he had been making at BYU. Community college positions may have been poor jobs, but they *were* jobs, after all. Quinn never held another permanent academic position and struggled to support himself financially for the rest of his life.

Perhaps not surprisingly, Quinn's separation from academia led to personal problems with his former academic associates. Of course, he remained on cordial terms with Arrington, but relations with others were strained to various degrees. One "seemed so guarded in phone conversations … that I decided to limit any inquiries to the 'safe' topic of computers," Quinn wrote to Arrington. A second former colleague was "so guarded that it appeared he was afraid I was going to circulate his letters, and recently he's adopted the silent approach." A third "has either not answered letters, or responded with restricted civility, or declined even to offer the suggestions or critiques I've invited on things I've already written. … In a way, I can understand all that. … But the faith and concerns which always motivated me as a Mormon historian are still operating within me.

---

69. Daniel Golden, "Expelled Scholar of Mormonism Can't Find Work," *Wall Street Journal*, Apr. 10, 2006; Stephen Speckman, "U. Professor Is in Hot Water," *Deseret News*, Feb. 7, 2004; Peggy Fletcher Stack and Linda Fantin, "Sparks Fly as U. Rejects an LDS Studies Scholar," *Salt Lake Tribune*, Feb. 6, 2004.

I always wrote on controversial stuff. I was good enough for their association once, and resent this personal dimension of the current Church situation."[70]

As if fate were not yet finished with Quinn, a greater tragedy still awaited him. His son Adam Darley Quinn, whom his father characterized as "a sensitive, passionate young man who enjoyed music, books, drawing, ideas, mountains, cooking, and his guitar," developed medical problems that were treatable, but only with consistent medication which he took inconsistently. When he was well, he did well indeed, making the Dean's List at Salt Lake Community College one year. Unfortunately, he was unwell much of the time. He became a drifter, traveling alone throughout the country. He was out of touch with his parents for long periods despite their offers of financial aid and pleas for phone calls. Tragedy struck in February 1996 when a hiker found twenty-one-year-old Adam's body hanging from a tree in a remote location in Salt Lake City's City Creek Canyon. The date of his death could not be precisely determined. Adam "has left us to explore other horizons," his grieving father wrote.[71]

From the 1990s until the end of his life, then, Quinn became, like his son Adam, a bit of a drifter. Cut off from his family, his academic position, and his church membership, there was little to hold him in any one place. Despite his ability to live frugally, financial problems dogged him constantly, at least until he was able to start drawing his small retirement pension from BYU and Social Security. Book royalties were never more than a fleeting windfall. He was able to land a one-year visiting lectureship at Yale—certainly the most lucrative of the several temporary positions he held. Otherwise, he flitted from one contract job to another—a gay-lesbian archives in southern California, editing an oral history collection at the University of Utah's Marriott Library. During the cold winter of 1999 he spent several months in Mexico, living rent-free in archivist Alfred Bush's condominium in Chiapas and taking largely futile lessons in Spanish, his father's native tongue. Upon his return, he was several

70. Quinn to Arrington, June 5, 1992, Arrington Papers.
71. Adam Quinn file in possession of Signature Books. Quinn, "Journal/Journey of a Gringo Chicano in Mexico," 1–2, in private possession, tells of Adam's troubled life. See also Philip Lindholm, ed, *Latter-day Dissent: At the Crossroads of Intellectual Inquiry and Ecclesiastical Authority* (Salt Lake City: Greg Kofford Books, 2011), 121–22.

thousand dollars in credit card indebtedness. When the 2006 *Wall Street Journal* article about his inability to find an academic position publicized his poverty, some of his friends attempted to create an endowment at a New Mexico bank to alleviate his financial distress, but it seems to have been only partially helpful.[72]

One bright spot in this otherwise depressing story is that eventually Packer's requirement that researchers in the church archives submit to censorship was lifted. That happy event was coupled with a new openness of access to archival records under administrators like Elder Marlin Jenson and Richard Turley, all of which added up to new research opportunities for historians like Michael Quinn. At the time of his death, Quinn was working on several extended projects, such as follow-ups to his same-sex dynamics book and his polygamy article.

Upon his return from Mexico, Quinn lived on a futon in his mother's condominium in Rancho Cucamonga, California, until her death, at which time the condo became his. He had been able to mend some of his relations with his father and enjoyed visits and telephone calls with him until he, too, died. Quinn tried to remain as good a father as he could, given the scattered nature of his family. He joined them as frequently as possible for holiday reunions and house-sat for Jan and her second husband when they were away.

Nevertheless, Quinn was alone in his condominium when he died from a heart attack on an undetermined date late in April 2021. His children had talked with him by telephone only a couple of weeks earlier, and they thought that he sounded fine. Quinn had always lived on the edge, personally, intellectually and ecclesiastically, and thus he had always been, in a sense, alone. So I wonder if there was perhaps something fitting in the fact that he died as he had lived.

---

72. Eugene Kovalenko, emails on file at Signature Books.

EPILOGUE

D. Michael Quinn's writings during what I have called his years of exile indicate that he had, to a high degree, come to peace with the tribulations and frustrations of his life. He and his father never became close, but they became as close as their vastly different personalities allowed. After his return from Chiapas in 1999, Quinn shared his mother's condominium and later inherited it. Divorce is rarely if ever easy, but he and Jan mutually recognized the necessity of their separation and did so amicably. "He wasn't always the parent we needed," his children remembered, but "he loved us tremendously. ... We miss him deeply."[1]

Although he came to characterize BYU—unfairly, in my view—as an "Auschwitz of the mind," he had good reasons for his frustration with the university administration's hypocrisy in pretending to maintain intellectual freedom while at the same time attenuating his. But he had had some happy years there and was popular with both his students and faculty colleagues. If some of the latter became cool toward him after his resignation and excommunication, Quinn understood that close association with him could be dangerous for them.

His excommunication was an especially cruel blow, but he never sought rebaptism and restoration of his membership because it would have required that he admit to wrongdoing. He had served his church well as a missionary, a temple worker, and in various local ward and stake callings and considered his insistence upon truth in his historical writings as the best service he could give to the LDS faith. He even gave a talk at a Sunstone symposium on "Why an

---

1. Michael Quinn obituary, *Salt Lake Tribune*, Apr. 26, 2021.

Excommunicated Mormon Historian Urges You to Remain *With* the LDS Church."[2]

And what of his scholarly achievement? Could he be at peace with that as well? The governing thesis in all of Quinn's work is the simple proposition that Mormonism, both theologically and institutionally, *has* a history.

Other proponents of the New Mormon History have been attacked by conservative readers both inside and outside the hierarchy of the Mormon Church. Their truth-telling, in fact, was the basic reason Leonard Arrington's History Division, of which Quinn had been a part, was banished to BYU in the early 1980s and access to the church archives severely restricted for the next two decades. Why was it, though, that Quinn's work in particular drew such violent protest and he himself was so savagely punished to the point of excommunication after having been, as he saw it, driven out of his academic position at BYU?

All religion may be seen as a combination of divine revelation and intervention on the one hand and of human agency on the other. The divine element, to an empirical historian, can never be verified, proven, nor demonstrated, whereas the human element is susceptible to all of those. Revelation may be claimed, but the only possible responses are acceptance or rejection depending on its credibility among its audience. The human element, though, as in all other human activities, can be documented and critically evaluated. Quinn, a man of deep faith who repeatedly and vigorously asserted that faith, nevertheless found it possible as a historian only to deal with the human elements in Mormon history and his critics chose, despite his repeated, articulate protestations to the contrary, to interpret him as saying that the human element is all there is to Mormonism.

The question remains, though, why Quinn was treated more harshly than his mentor Leonard Arrington and others of the New Mormon Historians? *Great Basin Kingdom*, Arrington's masterpiece and the fountainhead of the New Mormon History, studiously avoids any consideration of the validity of Mormonism itself, in stark contrast with the older Mormon histories of the likes of Joseph

---

2. Sunstone Symposium, Salt Lake City, July 31, 2014, transcript in possession of Signature Books Publishing, Salt Lake City.

Fielding Smith, which regarded history as a testing ground of that validity. Arrington simply told, as objectively as he could, what the Mormon Church and its members had done in the way of economic institutions and activity from 1830 to 1900. Failures were even included in his narrative: the United Order of Enoch was a mixed success at best, and some of the church's colonizing ventures were either failures or near-failures. But the basic impression one gets from Arrington's book is a story of impressive achievements through considerable suffering and against fearful odds.

Quinn, on the other hand, with his obsessively energetic research and inflexible honesty and objectivity in reporting his findings, did not shrink from venturing onto territory hitherto abandoned by many Mormon historians as the province of apostates and anti-Mormons bent on embarrassing the church. In perhaps his most impressive book, he offered elaborate documentation of the profound and pervasive influence of magic and other occult influences on the creation and early history of Mormonism. He discovered and bravely reported documentation of many dozens of polygamist marriages not only condoned, but actually performed, by general authorities of the church long after it had ostensibly abandoned the practice. He could even write about how "Mormon Women Have Had the Priesthood Since 1843." His immense trilogy on *The Mormon Hierarchy* tells a story of confusion, false starts, improvisation, and even revisions of Mormon scriptures as the church evolved from primitive beginnings to the elaborate, powerful, and wealthy organization it is today.

There may have been an underlying innocence and even a naïveté in Leonard Arrington's faith that honest and objective reporting of Mormon history would find an accepting and even enthusiastic reception among the Mormon public. That acceptance and enthusiasm were certainly there, but there was also an undercurrent of objection and resistance. Quinn's innocence and naïveté, I suggest, exists to a significant degree beyond Arrington's. Supported by an absolute integrity and honesty in presenting and defending his findings and supporting them with literally thousands of elaborate footnotes, it proved to be a lethal combination so far as his academic career and even membership in the church was concerned.

Other Mormon historians, including his admirers, have branded Quinn a "renegade" or a "maverick" historian. Quinn himself came to refer to himself an a "renegade" historian. For those of us on the outside, of both Mormonism and Mormon history, this seems a strange appellation. For our part, we are inclined to ask what precisely is "maverick" about Quinn's work. Wasn't he merely doing what all historians *should* be doing? Calling Quinn a maverick seems to many of us, instead, an indictment of his colleagues in the field who fall short of where they should be.

Could it be that the field of Mormon history has yet to become what Quinn already was? Some 300 years ago, the French *philosophe* Denis Diderot pointed to contemporary writers who were "too daring for the times in which their works appeared, [who] have been little read, hardly understood, not appreciated, and have long remained in obscurity, until the day when the age they had outstripped had passed away and another century, to which they really belonged in spirit, overtook them at last and finally gave them the justice their merits deserved." Pending the arrival of that day, perhaps Quinn's works may be provisionally vindicated anyway. "I have heard it said," Diderot continued, "that M. de Fontenelle's rooms were not large enough to hold all the works that had been published against him. Who knows the title of a single one of them"?[3]

In that vein, then, I wonder where Quinn's accusers are. Where are the FARMS "reviewers" who attacked the Mormonism and magic book viciously and groundlessly? Where is the assistant church historian who argued that Quinn's magic book should not be published—a book that went on to win the Mormon History Association's Best Book of the Year award? Where are the church officials, both general and local, who engineered and then, using others as proxies, carried out his excommunication? Is the LDS Church better, or worse, off for having rid itself of its arguably most courageously honest historian?

---

3. Denis Diderot, "Encyclopedie," in Isaac Kramnick, ed., *The Portable Enlightenment Reader* (New York: Penguin Books, 1995), 20–21.